Y0-CAN-856

# QUANTITATIVE METHODS IN BUDGETING

# Quantitative methods in budgeting

**Edited by**

C. B. Tilanus

Martinus Nijhoff Social Sciences Division
Leiden 1976

658.154
Q1

ISBN 90 207 0649 7

167405

Copyright © 1976 by H.E. Stenfert Kroese B.V., Leiden
No part of this book may be reproduced in any form by print,
photoprint, microfilm or any other means, without written
permission from the publisher

Photoset in Malta by Interprint (Malta) Ltd

Printed in the Netherlands by Intercontinental Graphics

# Contents

ABOUT THE AUTHORS  viii

1. INTRODUCTION
   C. B. *Tilanus, editor*  1

2. PEOPLE AND TECHNIQUES IN BUDGETING  10
   G. *Hofstede*
   2.1. The effectiveness of budget control systems 10
   2.2. The wood and the trees 11
   2.3. Potential psychological gains in using quantitative
        methods 14
   2.4. Quantitative methods in assessing the social aspects of
        a control system 18
   2.5. Conclusion 20

3. BALANCED TRANSFER VALUES IN SCHEDULING, COSTING
   AND RECOMPENSING  23
   A. *Klein Haneveld*
   3.1. Extended introduction and summary 23
   3.2. Linear programming and accountancy 26
   3.3. Models of the values as well as the measures of flows 28
   3.4. Linking objects: transferrers of value 32
   3.5. Balancing procedures: evaluation of intracompany trade 39
   3.6. Degrees of freedom and channels of valuation 47
   3.7. Ancillary interrelations in costing and recompensing 51
   3.8. Recapitulation 64

4. RATIO NETWORK MODELS AND THEIR APPLICATION IN
   BUDGETING  67
   C. *van der Enden*
   4.1. Ratio network models 67
   4.1.1. Basic ideas 67
   4.1.2. Input data 70
   4.1.3. Dimensions 71
   4.1.4. Relationships 72
   4.1.5. Application 74

4.2. Budgeting with the help of the ratio network
     method                                                             78
4.2.1. Introduction                                                     78
4.2.2. Management activities                                            80
4.2.3. The budget: basic ideas                                          83
4.2.4. The budget: flow-chart                                          85


5. THE DEVELOPMENT OF A BUDGETING MODEL                                 92
   *H. A. Smits and P. A. Verheyen*
5.1. Introduction                                                       92
5.2. The preliminary phase                                             92
5.3. The conceptual side                                               93
5.4. The general model                                                 93
5.5. The first phase                                                   94
5.6. The second phase                                                  95
5.7. Conclusions with respect to the implementation                     96
Appendix 5.1. Mathematical description of the generalized
     model                                                              98


6. COST ACCOUNTING, PLANNING AND BUDGETING                             109
   *A. Bosman and J. L. Bouma*
6.1. Cost functions and product costing                                110
6.2. The relations between production centres                          115
6.3. Alternative production methods of economically
     homogeneous products                                              118
6.4. Planning, linear programming and unit costs                       120
6.5. Planning, budgeting and costs                                     125
6.6. Example                                                           130


7. STOCHASTIC BUDGETING                                                135
   *T. Kloek and H. A. van der Donk*
7.1. Introduction                                                      135
7.2. Probability distributions                                         136
7.3. Some specific distributions                                       138
7.4. Relations between the variables                                   139
7.5. Computer program                                                  140
7.6. Interval boundaries and policy                                    142
7.7. Concluding remarks                                                143
Appendix 7.1. Flow-chart of computer program                           144
Appendix 7.2. Interval exploitation budget                             145
Appendix 7.3. A definition of subjective probability                   146

8. VARIANCE ANALYSIS, FLEXIBLE BUDGETING AND
RESPONSIBILITY ACCOUNTING 147
*C. B. Tilanus and J. A. M. Theeuwes*
8.1. Classical variance analysis 147
8.2. The flexible-budgeting approach to variance analysis 149
8.3. Multi-stage, multidimensional variance analysis 151
Appendix 8.1. Two-stage, two-dimensional variance analysis
with flexible budgeting 155
Appendix 8.2. Algebra and numerical example of two-stage,
three-dimensional variance analysis with flexible
budgeting 156

9. WHERE SHORT-TERM BUDGET MEETS LONG-TERM PLAN 159
*C. B. Tilanus*
9.1. Next year's budget in conflict with first year of long-
term plan 160
9.2. Using budget pattern for disaggregation of long-term
plan 160
9.3. The multiproportional RAS algorithm 164
9.4. Taking account of prior information 166

INDEX 169

# About the authors

*A. Bosman*
Born 1930. Master's degree in economics 1955; worked in industry until 1962; 1962–1968 director of the Institute of Economic Research of the University of Groningen; 1968 associate professor in management science; 1969 Ph.D. thesis on Systems, planning, networks; 1970 professor in management science; is especially interested in the problem area of constructing management information systems.

*J. L. Bouma*
Born 1934. Education: economic science, University of Groningen. Dissertation: A comparative study of theories of business behaviour (in Dutch), 1966. Author of some textbooks on managerial economics and finance. Present research: information and decision systems in an organization, management control systems.

*H. A. van der Donk*
Born 1937. Obtained degrees in economics as of 1967, in statistics as of 1971. Since 1968 employed as economics assistant at Netherlands Railways, Department of Research and Planning, Utrecht.

*C. van der Enden*
Born 1922. Education: Free University, Amsterdam, Faculty of Economics. Publication: Decision Calculations (in Dutch), 1975. Function: Head of the Industrial Economics Research Department of N. V. Philips' Gloeilampenfabrieken, Eindhoven.

*G. Hofstede*
Born 1928. Master's level degree in Mechanical Engineering from Delft Institute of Technology (1953) and Doctorate in Social Psychology from Groningen University (1967). Doctoral dissertation: 'The Game of Budget Control'. Current activities: Professor of Organizational Behaviour, European Institute for Advanced Studies in Management, Brussels, and Affiliate Professor, INSEAD, Fontainebleau, France. Earlier work experience: ten years in the Netherlands as an industrial worker, engineer, foreman and department manager, six years of behavioural research on the international staff of IBM-Europe, and two years of teaching at IMEDE, Lausanne. Publications, research interest, teaching and consulting activities all related to the impact of the design of large organizations on the behaviour of their members. Present research about the impact of national culture on organizational behaviour.

*A. Klein Haneveld*
Born 1915. Graduated 1937 in Electrical Engineering at Delft. Had a career of 32 years with the Royal Dutch/Shell. Until 1956 as a geophysicist, mainly in

South American countries. Thereafter successively Operations Superintendent of an oil field, head of a Computer Development group, and manager of Data Processing in Venezuela. From 1962 to 1969 senior adviser with the central Management Services at London and The Hague, concerned with investment criteria, planning procedures, and optimization techniques. Since 1970 teacher of Quantitative Methods in Business, at the Twente University of Technology, Enschede.

## T. Kloek
Born 1934. Ph.D. in economics, 1966, Netherlands School of Economics (now Erasmus University), Rotterdam. Subject of dissertation: Index Numbers (in Dutch). Joined the Econometric Institute at Rotterdam in 1959. Professor of econometrics in the same school since 1967. Coauthored (together with H. Theil and J. C. G. Boot): 'Operations Research and Quantitative Economics, An Elementary Introduction' (1965). Published several articles in Econometrica and other econometric and statistical journals. Current subject of interest: nonlinear estimation and its applications.

## H. A. Smits
Born 1914. Obtained a degree in economics at Tilburg University. Staff member of the Systems Department at Dutch States Mines (DSM).

## J. A. M. Theeuwes
Born 1944. Is a certified accountant, educated at Tilburg University, Department of Economics. He is Assistant Professor of Accounting at Eindhoven University of Technology. Author of various papers published in Dutch accounting journals. His current research interests are in the field of management information systems.

## C. B. Tilanus
Born 1936. Education: economics and econometrics. Thesis on 'Input-output experiments'. Worked with Theil at Econometric Institute, Netherlands School of Economics. Industrial experience in chemical and software industries. At present Associate Professor in quantitative economic methods at Department of Industrial Engineering, Eindhoven University of Technology. A founding editor of the European Journal of Operational Research (first volume 1977). Current interests: linear programming, management games, and the subject matter of this book.

## P. A. Verheyen
Born 1931. Education: 1953–1958, Econometrics, Tilburg University. Dissertation: Economics and technics (in Dutch), 1961. Functions: 1959–1966: (Coordinator of) Department of Statistics, Dutch States Mines; 1962–1966: Extraordinary Lecturer/Professor, Tilburg University; 1966–present: Professor, Tilburg University; 1968–1971: Dean of the Faculty; 1971–1973: Member of the Board of the University. Publications: About input-output analysis (inaugural lecture, 1967), investment planning (1975), and budget-model for a hospital (1975).

# 1. Introduction

C. B. TILANUS, EDITOR

This book tries to strengthen the ties between, on the one hand, the business administration and accounting world and, on the other, the operational research and management science world. The readership for which it is intended consists of the following categories: managers and professionals in organizational departments of business administration, management science, automatic data processing, etc.; management and operational research consultants; and students in academic departments of business administration, business economics, operational research, information systems, industrial engineering, etc.

The book deals with the quantitative approach to budgeting problems. Budgeting in this text is defined as the making of a *financial, short-term plan for an organization*. The budget is *financial*. Although volumes and prices play their part, the budget is finally expressed in terms of amounts of money thus allowing of the well-known two-way counting and balancing of double bookkeeping. (Whether items appear twice on the assets and liabilities sides of balances, or are counted twice in the rows and columns of a matrix is immaterial.) The budget is *short-term*. It is a detailed, quantitative plan of action in the near future. In this sense, budgeting is opposed to strategic planning which considers the course of action to be taken in the medium and long term. Strategic planning is of a more aggregative, qualitative nature than is budgeting. The budget is a plan for an organization, and as such it is *complete*. If the amount of planning information is measured on the vertical axis and time on the horizontal axis of a two-dimensional graph, the budget is a vertical slice from the graph. Techniques that would involve a horizontal slice from the graph, like investment analysis or capital budgeting and the planning, programming and budgeting system (PPBS) are outside the scope of this book.

If an organization has no budget, it makes no sense to consider quantitative methods. The situation that there is no budget may be more wide-spread among organizations and more recent in the past of other organizations than one may think. Moreover, the budget must be 'in the computer' in order to make the quantitative methods of more than theoretical interest. A budget that is in the computer is still outright uncommon. This is true even after a long time-span of relatively (and even absolutely) falling prices for automatic data processing equipment. Many organizations that are electronically well equipped and have to a large extent computerized the (ex post) registration side of their administration have not yet done so on the (ex ante) planning side.

There are three points, however, that brighten the outlook of the practical relevance of quantitative methods in budgeting.

1. Once the budget is computerized, soon the more sophisticated quantitative methods will become of interest. But there is a much stronger argument working in favour of computerization of the budget than just the application of quantitative methods. This argument is the shortening of the budgeting cycle time. I know of a firm in which the budget is hand-made by a few dedicated people from the administration department in a long sequence of talks with people from other departments. In June–July of a given year, sales plans and forecasts for the next year are collected from the sales departments. In September–October, sales figures are matched by production plans of the various (consecutive) production departments. In November and at the beginning of December, estimates of the indirectly productive and service departments are added. In three weeks of hard work around Christmas and at the beginning of January, the budget is totalled, checked and edited once and for all, and around the middle of January the 300-page volume is put into the cupboard once and for all. How could the budget actually be used, since the most important sales contracts are drawn up in the late autumn and everybody knows that sales prospects as of June, on which the budget is based, may have become completely unrealistic in January? If the budgeting process were computerized, the whole cycle could be accomplished in a matter of weeks. Data collection could proceed simultaneously, rather than sequentially, although more people would need to be put to work on the side of the administration department. Data collection would not consist in processing by hand numerical data on sales forecasts, via numerical estimates of production and overhead departments, until numerical final results were obtained. Data collection would rather consist in assessing functional relationships in mathematical or tabular form. These formulae or tables would allow of so-called flexible budgeting. *Computerizing* the budget means *functionalizing* the budget. If the budgeting process is computerized, there will even be hopes of making it a truly cyclical and iterative procedure: if management is not satisfied with the financial outcome, the budget can be revised, and revised again, in a converging process and will still be ready in time in January to be actually used as a tool and a target in the organization. Also, the budget can actually be updated: if in the course of the year to which the budget applies sales prospects change significantly, the budget can be revised and made realistic again. All this can only be done if the time needed for processing, checking and editing the budget data has dwindled to a few days or hours, i.e., if the budget is computerized.

2. The second favourable point is the fact that people in business are becoming more and more inclined towards quantitative methods in budgeting. The expansion of automatic data processing greatly enhances a positive attitude and interest in quantitative methods. Moreover, education in ever more disciplines is becoming ever more quantitative. For instance, business administrators and economists will attend courses in statistics, linear algebra, etc., at their university. Linear programming is shifting out of the realm of operational research into the realm of economics. [And rightly so, for is the linear programming problem not pre-eminently the basic economic problem in its alternative formulations, viz., maximizing ends for given means, or minimizing means for given ends?] Ever more business administrators will prefer written presentations of certain topics using matrix algebra to long and tedious verbal or numerical descriptions. They find that shorthand matrix notation facilitates thinking and writing about these topics rather than making it more difficult. [In this book, matrix notation is used freely as the need arises. Consequently, some chapters use no matrix notation and hardly any mathematics at all, whereas the presentation of others is mainly based on matrix notation. It was not deemed expedient to increase by one the number of elementary introductions to matrix notation in this text.]

3. Lastly, there is a point in expecting to come across interesting quantitative methods in budgeting especially in the Netherlands. The business climate in this country is decisively influenced by some very large firms. In the *Fortune* August 1975 list of the fifty largest industrial companies in the world, the jointly British and Dutch companies of Royal Dutch/Shell and Unilever rank second and eleventh, respectively, and Philips' Gloeilampenfabrieken ranks sixteenth. The list of the 300 largest industrial corporations outside the U.S. includes the following Dutch or semi-Dutch companies (with rank numbers): Royal Dutch/Shell (1), Unilever (4), Philips' Gloeilampenfabrieken (5), AKZO (42), ESTEL (45), DSM (71), Rhine-Schelde-Verolme (206), Esso Nederland (234). Moreover, the Dutch are a neat and orderly people. They like to have tidy administrations just as they have a tidy country. They may even compile budgets just for the fun of it (as has been described by Hofstede in chapter 2). There is certainly good reason to expect to find in this country pioneering studies in quantitative methods in budgeting that may gradually find wider application.

The order of presentation of the following chapters is, roughly, one of increasing generality and, in a sense, from the past and the present into the future. I have looked for interesting, new quantitative methods in budgeting that would already have proved their value in practical applications. If no regular practical application was found, I looked for a practical pilot study in industry. In case no pilot study was available but there were hopes that in future the method might prove to be of practical relevance, a fictitious numerical example was resorted to.

In the following paragraphs, the reader may find some notes on the historical background and the relative position of each contributed paper in this book. Needless to say, the authors retain full authority and responsibility regarding their own contributions.

*People and techniques in budgeting* (Chapter 2, by G. Hofstede)

In this chapter, Hofstede places a warning sign for the road ahead. He stresses the need not to overlook the wood of the budget in the context of the organizational socio-technical system for delight of handling the trees of quantitative techniques. Budgeting techniques are a condition sine qua non – a necessary but by no means sufficient condition for budgeting to be a useful management tool. This chapter is also an illustration of quantitative (statistical) methods applied to the social side of the budget. It is based on over 10 years of empirical studies.

*Balanced transfer values in scheduling, costing and recompensing* (Chapter 3, by A. Klein Haneveld)

Since all company budgets finally result in balances of money amounts, budgeting is faced with the intrinsic measuring problem of assessing values for all goods and services involved. This problem is more formidable if the company is large and decentralized and if the goods and services are not sold on an external market. We then have the problem of internal transfer pricing. Klein Haneveld has been dealing with this problem at Royal Dutch/Shell. The method he has developed is based on many years' experience and focuses on internal bargaining as the best possible substitute for competitive pricing in the market place.

*Ratio network models and their application in budgeting* (Chapter 4, by C. van der Enden)

In the early sixties, Van der Enden proposed the ratio network method for budgeting to the management of a Philips company. The method was a success, mainly because of its clarity and practicality. By now, ratio network models are applied on a wide scale throughout Philips, not only for budgeting but also for long-term planning and investment analysis. [They are known at Philips as GAMMA models which is an acronym from Group for the Application of Mathematical Methods in Administration.] The acceptance both by management and by the users has been achieved by a thorough introduction with a minimum of mathematics. The basic idea is that ratios between variables are more stable than the variables themselves.

A *ratio* ($r_{ij}$) explains one variable ($x_i$) in terms of another ($x_j$). If the variables are ordered consecutively (from $n$ to 1),

$$x_i = r_{i,i+1} x_{i+1} + b_i \qquad (1.1)$$

where a constant term $b_i$ has been added (which will in many cases be zero). In a ratio *network* model, which is a directed graph without cycles, there may be branchings of arrows in nodes (i.e., number of outgoing arrows or 'out-degree' > 1) and/or meetings of arrows in nodes (i.e., number of incoming arrows or 'in-degree' > 1). Hence, several variables may be explained by one other variable,

$$
\begin{aligned}
x_i &= r_{i,i+1} x_{i+1} + b_i \\
x_h &= r_{h,i+1} x_{i+1} + b_h \qquad h < i
\end{aligned}
\qquad (1.2)
$$

and/or one variable may be explained by several others,

$$x_i = r_{i,i+1} x_{i+1} + \ldots + r_{i,i+k} x_{i+k} + \ldots + b_i \qquad (1.3)$$

If the ratio network model is viewed as a linear model,

$$A x = b \qquad (1.4)$$

then the matrix of coefficients $A$ may be characterized as a band matrix, with ones on the main diagonal, ratios $-r_{i,i+1}$ on the first diagonal to the right of the main diagonal (some of them may be zero), sparse ratios $-r_{i,i+k}$ to the right of the band accounting for branchings and meetings, and zeroes for the rest:

$$
A = \begin{bmatrix}
1 & -r_{1,2} & & & & \\
 & 1 & -r_{2,3} & & \text{sparse off-band ratios} & \\
 & & \ddots & & & \\
\text{zeroes} & & & 1 & & -r_{n-1,n} \\
 & & & & & 1
\end{bmatrix}
\qquad (1.5)
$$

*The development of a budgeting model* (Chapter 5, by H. A. Smits and P. A. Verheyen)

This chapter describes the practical case of the development of a budgeting model at DSM (Dutch States Mines). It has been developed very gradually over a period of more than ten years. At DSM the happy circumstances occurred that the evolution of the budgeting model was in a harmonious pace with both the acceptance throughout the organization and the increase of computer capacity.

Initially, use was made of the so-called *roll-up system*. This implies that departments can be placed in a consecutive order. Deliveries of goods and services between departments are one-way ('forward') only. Thus the budgeting model is a recursive model which can be solved by successive substitutions starting from the last department. The model is also linear. Denoting the coefficients by $a_{ij}$ we can successively compute the variables $x_i, i = n - 1, n - 2, \ldots, 1$, from

$$x_i = a_{i,i+1} x_{i+1} + \ldots + a_{in} x_n + b_i \tag{1.6}$$

since the variables with higher indices on the right hand side have been computed in previous steps. If the roll-up technique is represented by a linear model (1.4), then the matrix of coefficients is triangular

$$A = \begin{bmatrix} 1 & -a_{12} & -a_{13} \cdots \cdots -a_{1n} \\ & 1 & -a_{23} \cdots \cdots -a_{2n} \\ & & \qquad \ddots \qquad \vdots \\ & \text{zeroes} & \qquad -a_{n-1,n} \\ & & \qquad\qquad 1 \end{bmatrix} \tag{1.7}$$

There is no essential difference in the matrix structure of the ratio network model and the roll-up technique. The way in which both methods have been presented and introduced in the respective organizations is, however, essentially different. Roll-up is the first step leading to a greater generality of representation and to the use of the matrix concept in thinking about budgeting.

In the course of some years, the budgeting model of DSM has developed into a full-fledged *input-output model* (1.4) where the so-called Leontief matrix has the structure

$$A = \begin{bmatrix} 1 & -a_{12} \cdots\cdots\cdots\cdots\cdots -a_{1n} \\ -a_{21} & 1 & \cdots\cdots\cdots -a_{2n} \\ \vdots & & \ddots & \vdots \\ & & & -a_{n-1,n} \\ -a_{n1} & -a_{n2} \cdots\cdots -a_{n,n-1} & 1 \end{bmatrix} \tag{1.8}$$

We now have a system of $n$(= hundreds or thousands of) simultaneous equations in $n$ unknowns the unique solution of which is found by matrix inversion

$$x = A^{-1} b \qquad (1.9)$$

As far as I know, the DSM input-output model is the only model of this type regularly used for budgeting in the Netherlands. [I know of several pilot studies which may eventually develop into integrated budgeting techniques.]

*Cost accounting, planning and budgeting* (Chapter 6, by A. Bosman and J. L. Bouma)

Since, as a rule, there is a choice between alternative ways of producing given end products, it would seem natural to expect applications of *linear programming* in budgeting. In a linear programming model, the A-matrix (see (1.4)) is rectangular – there are fewer equations than unknowns. It is well known that the problem of selecting a 'best' solution from the infinitely many solutions to (1.4) is solved by the simplex method, which maximizes a linear objective function in the unknowns

$$\max! \; x_0 = c_1 x_1 + \;\; \ldots \;\; + c_n x_n \qquad (1.10)$$

at the same time satisfying the equation system (1.4) (and the natural non-negativity constraints $x_i \geqq 0, \; i = 1, \ldots, n$).

I have found one integrated application of linear programming in budgeting in the Netherlands (in a Unilever plant) but there was no opportunity of getting a case report. There have been quite a few pilot studies. Although Bosman and Bouma have been involved in several studies, the quantitative side of this article is based on a numerical example only. The article has, however, a much wider scope. The authors deal extensively with the concepts used in accounting and budgeting. This discussion may be of particular interest to Anglo-American readers since their customs differ from those adhered to on the European continent.

*Stochastic budgeting* (Chapter 7, by T. Kloek and H. A. van der Donk)

This is the first chapter in which the uncertainty inherent in the forecasting of future events is incorporated into the budgeting method. The budgeting model is, in principle, stochastic and non-linear. The technique employed is simulation in order to obtain probability distributions of budget results based on subjective probability estimates of budget data. The budget thus becomes the mixed result of planning and forecasting elements.

The article is based on a prolonged pilot study carried out at Netherlands Railways. Special attention is paid to the possible impact of the 'probabilization' of the budget on the behaviour of the budgetee.

*Variance analysis, flexible budgeting and responsibility accounting*
(Chapter 8, by C. B. Tilanus and J. A. M. Theeuwes)

This chapter also deals with a non-linear budgeting model. Flexible budgeting indicates that budget items are, in principle, general (known) functions of production levels. This includes fixed cost items and (proportionally) variable cost items as special cases. The article looks specifically at the past: after the year for which the budget has been made has elapsed, variance analysis breaks down the differences that have arisen between budgeted and realized items. The article presents one general formula for breaking down variances which is justifiable in the (usual) case of a recursive cost model.

I regret to say that this article has failed to meet one of the objectives of this book, viz. that the methods described should have at least one practical application. Instead, the method is illustrated by a numerical example. The authors are still looking for an opportunity to apply it in a pilot study. The difficulty is that flexible budgeting is still very rarely applied. Flexible budgeting is a prerequisite for the general formula of variance analysis to be of interest. In the ordinary situation in which only the two categories of fixed and (proportionally) variable costs are distinguished the formula is trivial.

*Where short-term budget meets long-term plan* (Chapter 9, by
C. B. Tilanus)

This chapter specifically looks into the (farther) future. It is assumed that the budget is made bottom-up, as an extrapolation of the latest information on realized figures. Parallel with the budgeting activity, long-term planners, elsewhere in the organization, will make a top-down long-term plan derived from long-term objectives of the firm. The long-term plan is extrapolated backwards. The first year of the long-term plan coincides with the budget. In general, the two will *not* tally. They can be made consistent in three steps:
1. Compare the budget and the first year of the long-term plan and establish the differences
2. Confront budgeters and long-term planners with each other and let them try to resolve inconsistencies by judgement
3. Resolve any remaining inconsistencies in a suitable systematic way.
A suitable method is presented for resolving any remaining inconsistencies, on the assumption that overall aggregate figures are best established in the

top-down long-term plan, whereas the detailed pattern of relative figures is best established in the bottom-up budget. It is called the *multiproportional RAS* method. Again, I have not succeeded in performing a pilot study to try out this method. In an investigation currently carried out about long-term planning habits in the Netherlands, the first impression is that in most cases steps 1 and 2 in the confrontation between budget and long-term plan are not even taken. As long as this is the situation, we must postpone our hope of implementing step 3 into the future.

A *summary sketch* of our notes about the various contributions to this book and the order in which they have been placed is given in table 1.1. Naturally, this table can only give some bare bones of the articles. The reader is therefore cordially invited to savour the meat of the articles themselves.

*Table 1.1.* Characterization of contributions to this book.

| Chapter | technique involved | model matrix | application | firm |
|---|---|---|---|---|
| 2 | statistics | not applicable (n.a.) | pilot studies | various |
| 3 | bargaining | n.a. | integrated | Royal Dutch/ Shell |
| 4 | ratio network | band + sparse elements on one side | integrated | Philips |
| 5 | { roll-up | triangular | integrated | DSM |
| | input-output | square | integrated | DSM |
| 6 | linear programming | rectangular | num. example | n.a. |
| 7 | simulation | n.a. | pilot study | Neth. Railways |
| 8 | break-down | n.a. | num. example | n.a. |
| 9 | multiproportional RAS | n.a. | num. example | n.a. |

# 2. People and techniques in budgeting

G. HOFSTEDE

## 2.1. THE EFFECTIVENESS OF BUDGET CONTROL SYSTEMS

In 1964 and 1965, I studied budget systems in five well-organized companies in the Netherlands – the methods and procedures used, the information produced, and the impact of the system on the organization and its members. I started from the preamble that budgeting is meant to be an active process – it should affect the way the business is run, and for the better. The effectiveness of a budget system, then, should be measured through its impact on the efforts of the organization members to achieve better economic results. I avoid relating it directly with results itself, because results depend on many other things besides budgeting.

The conclusions of my study[1] (which focused on operating budgets rather than capital budgets and on manufacturing units rather than sales or administrative units), were that the effectiveness of a budget system relates to a limited extent only to the methods and techniques used in the budgeting process. It is important that the methods and techniques used be matched with the technical competence of the budget department, so that the system can be operated smoothly. The methods should allow budgets to be ready in time (that is, before the new budget year begins, which is often not the case), and variance reports should be produced regularly, timely and with few errors. If budget revisions are frequent, there should be a way to handle these with minimal disturbance of the system. However, within these rather obvious constraints different methods of budgeting appeared to function equally well. For example, of the five companies studied, three used a method in which individual plant departments were handled as full profit centers buying from and selling to each other (the 'European' method). The other two used a method in which only the (indirect) expenses of the plant departments were budgeted but in which direct production costs were handled through standard costing, outside the budget system (the 'American' method). Both methods had identifiable advantages and disadvantages but the effectiveness or ineffectiveness of the budget system was only marginally affected by the choice of method. What really made the difference in determining the effectiveness of the budget system in the companies I studied was the way the budget was used by operating management, because the managers – especially those at the middle and lower levels –

were the people who had to be motivated to act on the budget information for the system to be effective. The crucial problems were communication problems, between the budget department and operating management but even more within the management hierarchy itself. A budget is unavoidably a yardstick of managerial performance and the communication pattern that develops between the budgetee (the manager responsible for a budget) and his direct superior determines whether the budgetee will take this yardstick seriously, whether he will apply it to himself or try to escape its use by playing company politics. Even as far as the communication between the budget department and operating management goes, the bottleneck is more likely the person-to-person verbal communication than the written part of it, in the form of budget variance reports and the like. The conclusion of my study can be summarized in a few words: budgeting is much more than an administrative technique – it is a way of managing. The key role in a budget system is taken by the top line management – the role of the controller and of his budget department is auxiliary. In modern organization jargon, a budget system is a socio-technical subsystem of the organization which it tries to control and which itself is a more complicated socio-technical system. It appears that the trouble with budget systems is more often in the social than in the technical processes involved.

It may be that the particular sample of five Dutch companies used by me and the time at which the study was done (1964–65) affected the results to the extent that my conclusions do not apply for most other situations. However, both older and more recent[2] publications from the U.S.A. report similar results and discussions with managers from different countries who attended my classes in executive development courses do confirm that the trouble with budget control systems is more often in their use than in the methods and techniques followed.

2.2. THE WOOD AND THE TREES

Now all this does not mean that the issue of budgeting methods and techniques is unimportant. Budget control systems do need good techniques in order to function at all. However, well-chosen techniques, efficiently administered, do not guarantee an effective budget control system, if line management does not use the system properly. Poorly chosen or poorly administered techniques, on the other hand, do guarantee the failure of a system. The role of the techniques – and, more in general, the role of the controller's department in budgeting – is therefore 'hygienic'. Like in the case for hygiene in relationship with health, techniques in budgeting are a necessary but not sufficient condition. In fact, focusing too much on techniques in a budget control system may do harm, because it makes the system less understandable for the executives and managers who should be the main users. In one company, there was a very complete data collection system for budget variances. The budget department monthly produced a report based on these data and containing 19 different well-designed tables and graphs. I asked line managers which of these they usually read. Only 3 out of the 19 were read by more than 25% of the interviewees. Now over-information has the effect of limiting a person's ability to distinguish what is important in a message; it is the 'noise' that detracts from the 'message'. The error made by the budget department in this case was to assume that because the 19 tables could technically be reported, they should be reported. One budget analyst in this case commented that line management could not see the wood for the trees, but I think it is first of all the budget department which did not see the wood (the purpose of a budget control system) for the trees (the available techniques).

In another company, budget variances were reported monthly, divided into volume variances and other variances. Volume variances are those gains or losses in comparison with the budget which are caused by a larger or smaller sales and/or production volume than foreseen in the budget, which leads to an over- or under-absorption of fixed costs. Other variances include efficiency variances (due to a greater or smaller technical efficiency in the use of direct labor and direct materials), expense variances (due to differences in unit costs or overhead expenses), and accounting system variances (due to changes in accounting procedures). The distinction between these types of variances is essential for line management to understand the causes of gains and losses shown. However, in the particular company studied, *none* of the first or second line management receivers of the budget variance reports were able to explain the difference between volume and other variances. In this case the budget department had failed to insure that its techniques (in itself perfectly sound) were understood by those people whom these techniques were meant to serve. Again it saw the trees, but not the wood.

In modern organization jargon again, what often happens is a sub-optimization of the technical part of the budget control system, at the expense of the optimization of the entire (socio-technical) control system which does include things like the effective understanding and use of variance information by line management. Optimization of the socio-technical system, however, demands a general management rather than a functional-technical point of view. Unfortunately, our way of thinking is influenced by the work we do; people who have to do functional-technical work will think in a functional-technical way. One of the basic problems of organization is to integrate the efforts of groups of people who are induced by their task to think in different ways.[3] An illustration of the kind of differences in thinking between budget people and production managers can be found in a study I did among managers participating in executive development classes. Between 1970 and 1973, 372 managers from 40 countries at IMEDE Management Development Institute in Lausanne scored what they saw as their work-related values on a standard values test, L. V. Gordon's Survey of Personal Values.[4] Table 2.1 shows the scores of the 262 respondents of over 30 years of age divided according to the occupational area in which they had spent the past years of their career. The test is scored in such a way that the six dimensions together always add up to 90 points (an average of 15 points per dimension).

The two occupational groups with the most different scores are Finance (including Accounting and Efficiency experts) on the one side, and Engineers (including Production) on the other. In comparison with Engineers, Finance people scored *lower* on '*Practical Mindedness*' (defined as: to always get one's money's worth, to take good care of one's property, to get full use out of one's possessions, to do things that will pay off, to be very careful with one's money). Engineers scored *higher* on '*Variety*' (defined as: to do things that are new and different, to have a variety of experiences, to be able to travel a great deal, to go to strange or unusual places, to experience an element of danger). Engineers scored *lower* on '*Orderliness*' (defined as: to have well-organized work habits, to keep things in their proper place, to be a very orderly person, to follow a systematic approach in doing things, to do things according to a schedule). I believe that these systematic differences in how finance people and engineers described their own values, are reflected in organizations where people from the finance category act as budget experts and engineers act as production managers. Especially the trade-off between 'Orderliness' (sense of system, formalism) and 'Practical Mindedness' (what's the use of it?) is enlightening. These

*Table 2.1.* Mean scores on Survey of Personal Values for IMEDE respondents divided by occupation (age over 30 only).

| | Scores for occupation | | | |
|---|---|---|---|---|
| Test dimensions | Marketing $n = 72$ | Finance etc. $n = 66$ | Engineering $n = 48$ | General $n = 76$ |
| P – Practical Mindedness | 11.2 | 9.5† | 12.4† | 11.0 |
| A – Achievement | 19.3 | 19.4 | 18.7 | 19.0 |
| V – Variety | 11.1 | 9.6 | 12.8† | 10.0 |
| D – Decisiveness | 15.0 | 16.0 | 15.0 | 14.8 |
| O – Orderliness | 13.9 | 15.6 | 12.5† | 15.2 |
| G – Goal Orientation | 19.3 | 19.9 | 18.4 | 19.8 |

Scores with † are significantly different from those for the sum of all other occupations at a 5%-level (t-test, one-tailed).

differences in thinking do cause a 'differentiation' which, if not compensated by an 'integration' process, leads to the kind of malfunctioning of budget control systems pictured in the two examples above.

Now what happens if the budget department supplements traditional accounting methods by quantitative methods? If the difference in value systems between budget department and line management remains as it was, the transfer to quantitative methods risks to widen the gap between those designing and operating the budget machine and those supposed to use it. Quantitative methods in budgeting may lead to a new technical sub-optimization, more powerful than before, because it is now supported by more scientific methods, suggesting measurability and reliability. There is a general danger in management science that the mathematical techniques used to solve problems are more accurate than the data on which the solutions have to be based. There is a temptation to define problems in terms of the available solution – solution first, problem afterwards. This situation does apply strongly to budgeting where basic data are almost always not only imprecise but also biased by the interests of the people playing the budget game. With a new and shining machine to handle the trees some people may have even more difficulty in seeing the wood.

## 2.3. POTENTIAL PSYCHOLOGICAL GAINS IN USING QUANTITATIVE METHODS

The previous paragraphs may be seen as a call for modesty about the impact of quantitative methods on budget systems, and therefore they have stressed the negative aspects more than the positive ones. I have argued that a budget system is a socio-technical system. This implies that changing one element (in this case, an element on the technical side) potentially affects all others, including the social side. I have also argued that in most budget control systems the trouble is on the social side, and that one should avoid that the use of quantitative methods increases this trouble. The systems thinker will object now that I have assumed that a 'better' designed technical system inevitably leads to a worse designed socio-technical system (technical sub-optimization). He may argue that I have fallen into the same trap as those Human Relations theorists who believed that all control systems were inhuman.[5] The question is, whether the use of quantitative methods is really necessarily psychologically negative, or whether we, armed with both quantitative-technical and psychological insight, can design a socio-technical system which is integrally superior. Is there a way for quantitative methods to help there where the trouble is?

One problem preventing a better use of budget control systems is unrealistic assumptions about human behavior in both budget experts and line executives. In my book 'The Game of Budget Control' I have listed a number of assumptions evident from the classical accounting literature on budgeting.[6] Some of these are true to such a small extent that they must be considered as misleading:

- The only source of control is at the top of the organization; control lines flow from the top downward;
- The relationships of lower levels to higher levels in the organization can meaningfully be described in terms of accountability;
- The perfect manager manages by exception;
- People react on control systems as individuals (rather than as members of a reference group).

Some other assumptions about human behavior reflected in the accounting literature are true under certain, but not all conditions:

- Goal setting by the organization improves people's performance;
- Having people participate in this goal-setting improves their performance still more;
- People will take action when a deviation of an actual situation from a standard is reported to them.

An American study by Caplan[7] lists a much more extensive series of doubtful behavioral assumptions in the 'traditional' management accounting model of the firm contrasted with modern organization theory. In a field study of management accountants and line (non-accounting) managers, Caplan shows that most of the management accountants questioned tended toward the traditional view, and that the same was true for the non-accounting managers.

Now a system cannot function properly if it is based on untrue assumptions. So we should first of all replace the misleading assumptions by assumptions that are more true in the light of recent empirical research and modern organization theory:

- Control (in the sense of determining what actually goes on in the organization) is widely distributed among the members; however, different forms of control predominate at different levels and sections of the organization.
- People will take action only if they are motivated to act. They may be motivated indirectly – because by acting they expect to avoid a punishment or earn a reward – or directly, that is, because the particular act is intrinsically rewarding to them (it carries its psychological reward in itself). The trouble with indirect motivation is that it easily leads to

evasion: if people can avoid the punishment or earn the reward in another way than through acting, they may very well do so. For example, instead of trying to correct an unfavorable budget variance, managers may try to show why not they, but somebody else should be blamed for it.

- Accountability is psychologically related with punishment and more likely to lead to evasion than to motivation.
- Management by exception is psychologically highly undesirable because it leads to focus attention of superiors only on those aspects in the work of their subordinates that are wrong. It leads to a behavior of the superior which is seen by the subordinates as negative and punitive. It is, however, very seldom practised as traditional theory wants it.
- People in an organization mostly belong to one or more reference groups (for example, the group of supervisors, the group of Department A) and they will react to a control system in accordance with the subculture of their reference group which has developed over time and through experience.
- Goal setting by the organization will only lead to improved performance of people if the goals are 'internalized' by people and affect their performance aspiration levels.
- Participation by people in goal setting will only improve performance if people are motivated to set high targets for themselves. This will only be the case if they are directly motivated by the act of goal achievement. If goal achievement will lead to extrinsic reward or goal nonachievement to punishment, people will 'play it safe' and, in participating, bargain for goals that can be safely achieved but, by the same token, are less than challenging.
- Managers will only take action when a deviation of an actual situation from a standard is reported to them, if: they believe the information, they understand the information, they perceive it as relevant and attribute a sufficient priority to it, if effective action is technically possible, if they know how to take it, and if they can motivate the others involved (for example their subordinates) to cooperate in the action; finally, if they are not motivated to correct the deviation of actual from standard in a different way, for example by changing the data about the actual, changing the standard, or attributing the variance to somebody else.

There is no basic reason why, when assumptions about human behavior are corrected to be more realistic, the use of quantitative methods in budgeting should have exclusively dysfunctional effects on the social side of the system. One example of an area where quantitative methods in budgeting could be behaviorally functional is in the use of control limits in the statistical sense. Such control limits are common in quality control but rarely used in budgeting or cost control. Control limits define in advance a certain area of positive and negative budget variance which could occur either by random reasons, or else is consciously left to the discretion of the budgetee. The control limits are the quantitative expression of a 'planned area of free play' for the budgetees within the constraints of the overall budget. Miles and Vergin[8] list a number of features built into what they call 'variance controls' which make them look promising from a behavioral point of view:

1. They require an objective definition of performance standards, based on actual data.
2. They create a certain flexibility around standards.
3. They create control limits, within which the individual can establish his own performance targets.
4. They appear to have the potential for creating a positive atmosphere for the exercise of necessary corrective action; management's action can be viewed by both parties as problem-solving rather than punitive.
5. They are, potentially at least, both simple to apply and easy to understand.
6. Feedback can be both immediate and automatic.

The authors conclude that, 'variance controls appear to offer a potentially valuable compromise between traditional control techniques and the somewhat abstract and frequently vague control suggestions made by various behavioral scientists'.

In consolidating budgets with control limits into overall budgets, some assumptions should be built in about the probabilistic behavior of actual results within the limits. When a system of control limits is introduced, people may still be conditioned by previous experience to push their results to the upper expense limit. It may take time for people to learn to truly use the free area within the limits.

Another example where quantitative methods in budgeting can be behaviorally functional is in mathematical model building, to try to understand the effect of such phenomena as overall budget cuts (or other ways of increasing overall pressure) or (using mathematical game theory) of the negotiation process in budget setting. These models should of course take into account the social components in the system[9]. But in this case, a caution is due to maintain a healthy skepticism about the relationship between the models and reality – models tend to be so comfortable to work with that there is always a temptation to stop bothering about the reality they try to represent.

2.4. QUANTITATIVE METHODS IN ASSESSING THE SOCIAL ASPECTS OF A
CONTROL SYSTEM

One of the reasons why the technical side of a socio-technical system is
often sub-optimized at the expense of the social side, is that the first is
mostly tangible and measurable and the second not. The technical mind
has a tendency not to count with that what cannot be measured.

One answer to this problem is to make the social side of the system
more measurable. The 'intangibles' are often very tangible in their effects
and with proper methods of measurement, they can be made visible. This
means, combining the techniques of the social sciences (sociology, psychology) with the techniques of accounting, to assess the *integral* function-
ing of the socio-technical budget control system.

Social variables that can be measured are, for example, the motivation
of the budgetees by the budget variances that are reported to them; the
extent to which the information that is reported is understood, memorized,
and used by budgetees and others; feelings, psycho-somatic symptoms,
and behavioral symptoms of stress among budgetees and others; the frequency and emotional loading with which budget issues are discussed
between superiors and subordinates, between budgetees and budget
experts, and in various types of meetings; attitudes.to and behavior during
budget negotiations, including hedging against expected budget cuts;
degree of risk accepted in the setting of budget goals. This list can be
expanded at will. A number of these variables were measured in the study
of budget control systems in five Dutch companies described in my book
'The Game of Budget Control'. Some attempts at measuring social variables in this study were clearly more successful than others (some were
outright failures). One successful measurement can be described here as an
example. It deals with the *motivation of budgetees by the budget variances
reported to them*. ('The Game of Budget Control', page 156 ff.) This motivation will partly depend on the extent to which the budget is 'internalized'
by the budgetees. That is, to what extent the budgetees apply in their own
judgement of a situation the same yardstick as the budget. Let us take the
case of materials usage. For high motivation of the managers by the materials usage budget, it will be necessary that:

– if the (monthly or weekly) budget variance report shows a loss in materials usage, the manager will feel unhappy about his department's
  materials usage performance;
– if the budget variance report, however, shows a gain or a break-even the
  manager will feel happier.

On the contrary, if we find that:

– the managers' own feelings about how well their department is doing in
  materials usage does not at all correspond to the budget variance reports,

we can conclude that the motivation of the managers by this part of the
budget is low.

After all, we can only expect a manager to attempt taking action upon
a situation if he notices a disequilibrium: if he feels there is something
wrong. If he is convinced that things are as good as they can be (whatever
the budget variance report may say) he is unlikely to take any action.

These considerations led to a measurement technique consisting of
asking all managers to evaluate their own department's operation in a
number of aspects. These aspects were the 'measurable dimensions' of
their operation, basically the issues for which there were separate items
in their budget. These measurable dimensions fell into the following categories:

1. Efficiency of direct labor ('direct' meaning: immediately attributable to
   a certain product)
2. Efficiency of indirect labor
3. Machine hour efficiency
4. Efficiency of direct materials usage
5. Efficiency of the usage of indirect materials and tools
6. Extra costs resulting from rejection or re-work of products not meeting
   quality standards.

Every manager was now asked to rate his operation on each of those
'measurable dimensions' that applied to it, using a scale similar to the one
used in Dutch schools:

> 9 = excellent
> 8 = good
> 7 = fairly good
> 6 = satisfactory
> 5 = so-so

We can expect, that if budget motivation is high, a 'loss' in the variance
reports will correspond with a low self-rating of the manager (5 or 6), but
a 'gain' in the variance reports will correspond with a high self-rating of
the manager (8 or 9). In other words, in the case of 'high budget motivation'
there will be a *positive correlation* between the budget variance and the

manager's self-rating. If budget motivation is low, however, budget variance and self-rating will be unrelated.

In the 5 companies in which the research was carried out, 90 budgetees (line managers) supplied a total of 466 ratings of their performance, an average of just over 5 ratings (measurable dimensions) per budgetee. Each of these 466 ratings was then compared to the corresponding reported budget variance over the last available period. These budget variances were coded as follows:

$-2$: more than 5% loss
$-1$: 1–5% loss
    $0$: even ± 1%
$+1$: 1–5% gain
$+2$: more than 5% gain

The overall correlation coefficient between the managers' self-ratings and the budget variance (coded as described above) was 0.32[10]. A correlation coefficient of 1.00 would indicate perfect consistency between self-rating and budget variance; a correlation coefficient of 0.00 would indicate self-ratings totally unrelated to the budget. The figure of 0.32 means an in-between situation. However, this figure was not the same for each of the manufacturing plants studied (as in one of the five companies, two plants were studied, the total number of plants was six). The correlations between self-ratings and budget variance of the six plants were: 0.07; 0.16; 0.21; 0.28; 0.39; 0.41. For each plant, this correlation coefficient can be considered as an index of the motivation of the budgetees by the budget variances reported to them. If this index is low, for example below 0.20,[11] the budget variances do not motivate budgetees to take action. The higher it is, the more budgetees will be motivated to take action, if at least other circumstances do not prevent them from doing so. For a further discussion of this index, I have to refer the reader to 'The Game of Budget Control'.

This is just one example how quantitative methods can be used to assess the social part of the budget control system.

2.5. CONCLUSION

The considerations in this chapter lead to the following recommendations as to budget control policy:

– Budget control systems should not be made more sophisticated than their users.

- Technically better methods of budgeting should be tested on their effect on the users, in particular on the understandability of the information they generate, and on their motivational impact.
- The use of statistical control limits for budgets is worth considering and trying out. In this respect, budget experts can learn from quality control people.
- The social side of a budget system is often a more fruitful area to develop quantitative methods (measurements) for than the technical side. In this respect, budget experts can learn from social scientists.
- It is desirable to build into budget control systems periodic measures of their overall effectiveness including their impact on the social side of the organization.

The last point is just an application to budget control of a more general principle, that for any policy or system created by a manager, he should try to collect some kind of feedback as to its effectiveness in total system terms. A successful application of this principle is demonstrated in the following case, which may serve to conclude this chapter. It is not about budget control, however, but about the related issue of control by standard costs. A manufacturing plant had introduced standard costs in a number of its departments. A periodic employee attitude survey (measurement of the social side of the system) showed shortly afterwards a considerable lowering of the confidence of workers in their foremen. Rather than choose the typical solution of sending all foremen to human relations training, the personnel department analyzed the data further, and found that the confidence in the foremen had only dropped in those departments put on standard costs. Interviews showed that workers had lost confidence in their foremen, because foremen could no longer fix a man's production targets as they did before; these targets were now imposed by the engineers who set the standards used in the standard costs. The plant manager then decided to do an experiment: in some 'experimental' departments foremen obtained the right to reject standards which they considered unfair to their workers, however, the losses incurred by the rejection of standards were put on a special account for the foreman's department and so they were still visible. After four to five months, employee attitudes were measured again for both experimental departments and the other departments using standard costs; also, the productivity and quality performance of each department was followed. It appeared that in the experimental departments, confidence of employees in the foremen had been restored without any loss in productivity or quality. Seeing his diagnosis confirmed, the plant manager then gave to all foremen the right to reject standards considered unfair. This case[12] illustrates both the use of measurements on the social side of a system, and of a skillfully conducted experiment to quantitatively assess the effectiveness of a policy decision before making it general. It is an example of using quantitative methods there where the trouble is.

NOTES

1. Published in: G. H. Hofstede, *The Game of Budget Control*, Van Gorcum/Tavistock, 1967, 1972 and in: G. H. Hofstede, *Baas en Budget* (in Dutch), Samsom, 1968, 1974.
2. See for example: W. J. Bruns Jr. and D. T. De Coster (editors). *Accounting and its Behavioral Implications.* McGraw-Hill, 1969.
   R. N. Anthony, J. Dearden and R. F. Vancil, *Management Control Systems*, Irwin, revised edition 1972.
   A. G. Hopwood, *An Accounting System and Managerial Behaviour*, Saxon House/Lexington Books, 1973.
3. The concepts of differentiation and integration in organizations were brought to the fore in the work of Lawrence and Lorsch. For example, see P. R. Lawrence and J. W. Lorsch, *Organization and Environment: Managing Differentiation and Integration.* Harvard Business School, 1967.
4. This research is described in G. H. Hofstede, *Nationality and Espoused Values*, Working Paper 74-8, European Institute for Advanced Studies in Management, Brussels, March, 1974.
5. For an example of this kind of Human Relations thinking in the area of budgeting, see Chris Argyris, 'Human problems with budgets', *Harvard Business Review*, 1953 No. 1, 97–110. Argyris at this time did not recognize that budgets may also have positive motivational consequences.
6. *The Game of Budget Control*, p. 37.
7. E. H. Caplan, 'Behavioral assumptions of management accounting', *Accounting Review* 41(1966), 496–509, and 43(1968), 342–362.
8. R. E. Miles and R. C. Vergin, 'Behavioral properties of variance controls', *California Management Review*, 1966, 3, 57–65.
9. Examples of this can be found in: C. P. Bonini, 'Simulation of organizational behavior', in Bonini, et al., *Management Controls*, McGraw-Hill, 1964, and in E. B. Roberts, 'Industrial dynamics and the design of management control systems', in the same book.
10. The regression formula for the data from all 5 companies taken together was:
    $E = 0.29V + 7.3$ in which $E$ = manager's self-rating (5–9) and $V$ = budget variance; coded as described from $-2$ to $+2$.
11. For the numbers of observations used in my research, a correlation coefficient of 0.20 for a plant would be statistically significantly different from zero at about the 0.05 level.
12. Published at CEDEP-INSEAD, Fontainebleau, under the title 'The Case of the Disputed Standards' (1975).

# 3. Balanced transfer values in scheduling, costing and recompensing

## A. KLEIN HANEVELD

### 3.1. EXTENDED INTRODUCTION AND SUMMARY

The term transfer values is not common in the literature. The usual term is transfer prices, which are sums of money which one company division obtains from another division in exchange for a specified unit of a good or service. My reluctance to use the term prices dates from the time that I was an adviser on quantitative methods in the Central Offices of the Royal Dutch/Shell Group, from 1962 till 1969. Those were the days of enthusiastic and widespread development of linear programming models in Shell Operating Companies, accompanied by a growing concern at Central Offices about the validity of the money figures that comprised input and output of these submodels. Results from one submodel did not always fit in with those from another, and in order to thrash out discrepancies it became increasingly important to adhere to classic concepts and terminology. Commenting on these matters, one high official confided to me in despair: 'I wish everyone would understand the difference between values, costs and prices'. Transfer prices were per definition quoted on invoices. They were the result of discussions on the basis of operating plans that were made beforehand. They served within rather narrow limits to regulate the distribution of Group profit over its many affiliates, so that each of these affiliates showed a profit or loss which was commensurate with its commercial and political position. Different 'prices', for different purposes like scheduling, costing and recompensing, were unthinkable. One might differ of opinion about the relative position of the various affiliates, but not about the purpose of a transfer price. Once transfer prices were agreed upon for the next 3 or 6 months, they were not intended to generate a series of revisions to the various operating plans. Pricing followed scheduling, just like the costing of products is an exercise that by its very nature must be associated with a fixed schedule of operations. The same can be said of *recompensing*, a term which I use to describe the distribution of revenues minus expenses over various items of investment [4, 27, 1, 29].

In this paper I reserve the term transfer price for the sum of money that changes hands when goods or services flow from one corporate unit to an affiliated unit. I use the term value in a neutral sense, like many authors do, to describe any money amount that can be associated with property. Transfer values apply in particular to objects flowing from one division to other divisions, regardless of the question whether or not any one of these divisions is a separate corporate unit within the enterprise as a whole. An alternative term that I use is *flow values*. Transfer or flow values are intended to serve the individual divisions as yardsticks in their planning and accounting, so that these divisions are able to view their operations, revenues and expenses in a context that reflects the position of the enterprise as a whole. Transfer values are thus an instrument that makes decentralization possible [26, 15].

'Forcing' divisional managers to act in accordance with laid down policies, is often listed as the main function of a transfer pricing scheme. This premise leads to the awkward conclusion that divisional managers loose perforce their initially desired degree of autonomy. Many relatively simple examples are given in the literature to illustrate this point. In my personal experience, however, the problem is not so much that divisional managers are inclined to pursue sub-optimal objectives. The problem is really, how to translate overall objectives into terms that do apply to separate divisions, and are verifyable by divisional managers. There are fundamental difficulties in establishing costs of individual products, and identifying profitable areas of business, when the production system involves a complex network of co-production.

Costs and proceeds might be traced easily to individual activities. The difficulties arise when these money items are to be *reallocated*. Transfer values are treated in this paper as the instrument of reallocation. The system of measuring such transfer values for a particular accounting period depends on the purpose of the exercise, be it the scheduling of activities, the costing of products, or the recompensing of investments. In each of these cases the required set of transfer values will correspond to an equilibrium between internal supply and demand at the points of transfer. Hence the term *balanced* transfer values, a term which I will elaborate upon in this paper.

The reallocation of money values from one object to other ones implies the existence of a *numerical interrelation* between the measures of these objects, be they historic, contemporary or prospective measures. The recipients of the values can be looked upon as *calculation objects*, chosen in accordance with the purpose of the reallocation exercise:

    in scheduling    – strains (internal and external),
    in costing       – sales (external)
                       and inventories (internal or external),
    in recompensing  – investments (internal).

Scheduling can be looked upon as an exercise for the purpose of determining the optimal measures of flow within a given set of constraining conditions. The exercise shows, which internal and external strains are effective in the accounting period under consideration. In addition, it measures the net benefits achievable in the accounting period by loosening the strains. But this information is misleading, because the benefits are not exclusively related to objects that are external. Maximization of net income in an accounting period – a simplistic objective of scheduling – should be pursued as only a means to an end. The ends themselves should be external, because an enterprise needs external objectives in order to survive. Internal objects are important only because of their constraining effect on the pursuance of external objectives [19, 20].

Recompensing exercises – the measuring of earnings due to individual investments – are even more misleading than scheduling exercises, because of their exclusive concentration on internal objects. The recompensing of investments, like the valuation of internal strains while scheduling, highlights internal benefits of reduction and expansion. However, the external objectives and their associated internal sacrifices deserve even greater attention.

Ideally, every scheduling and recompensing exercise, whether retrospective or anticipatory, should be accompanied by a costing exercise. Valid and viable procedures of absorption costing are particularly desirable, in view of their relevance to long term aspects. Proponents of direct costing have been apt to loose sight of this fact [33, 31, 32].

The results of each exercise of scheduling, costing or recompensing are associated with a particular collection of calculation objects, and a consequent representation of numerical interrelations between volumes of flow, i.e. between measures of goods and services provided in the accounting period, and of raw materials and durable producer goods that are thereby sacrificed. In my opinion it is good practice to represent the real interrelations by linear ones within relevant ranges. Accountants have done so for ages. The availability of linear scheduling models and electronic computers ought to inspire them to continue this good practice in years to come.

The numerical interrelations between measures of flow are transformed, and if need be expanded, so that each one serves to specify how the nonzero measure of a particular *dependent activity* is uniquely defined by the measures of one or more calculation objects. The calculation objects themselves must not have a fixed relation, however. Their measures should be *independently variable* for the purpose of the exercise, whereas the measure of a dependent object should be variable only by one or more accompanying changes in the measures of the calculation objects. These are the conditions under which benefits and sacrifices can be *traced indirectly* to calculation objects, i.e. by re-allocation via numerical interrelations between measures of flow.

An exercise of scheduling, costing and recompensing does not produce 'decisions'. Decisions call for an assessment of relevant pros and cons. Models of flows of goods and services do not accomplish any assessment. Instead, they serve to measure sacrifices and benefits that are indirectly traceable to individual items in a collection of fairly independent calculation objects. The composition of such a set of separate objects is a matter of choice. Hence the general distinction between costing, scheduling and recompensing. The selection of relevant items of costs and revenues is again a matter of choice, affected by the question whether long term or short term aspects are under study. There is little leeway, however, in the selection of an appropriate *basis* for the reallocation of costs and revenues. The selection of this basis might involve the choice of by-products, by-investments and *ancillary calculation objects*, which are discussed in this paper. But in spite of the complications caused by these matters, there is good reason to believe that balanced transfer values enable divisional managers to view their operations in the desired context of the objectives of the enterprise as a whole.

Associated with a set of transfer values, one per location of transfer, is a set of *linking objects*, also one per location of transfer. A linking object is the measure of flow in one of the internal channels of supply and demand at the location of transfer. In the event that a scheduling, costing or recompensing exercise is done through the combined efforts of associated divisions, the linking object at a point of transfer becomes for the division to which it belongs an additional calculation object, with an independent measure and an *indifferent* net money value. No set of transfer values is complete without a corresponding set of linking objects. The two sets together give the divisions proof that their divisional measurements are valid for the enterprise as a whole.

This fundamental theory of transfer values and linking objects is further expanded and illustrated in the succeeding sections of this paper. Balanced transfer values and indifferent linking objects are the basic elements in planning and accounting procedures that are intended to help divisional managers in their efforts to pursue joint objectives. Any decentralized organization with overall objectives would benefit from a gradual build-up of practical experience in the application of these theoretical valuation tools.

## 3.2. LINEAR PROGRAMMING AND ACCOUNTANCY

Some 10 years ago, at the occasion of a conference of Shell operational research workers, I predicted that linear programming models would develop into powerful tools for cost accountants in the petroleum industry, and that these tools would continue to be used after more sophisticated models might be developed for the purpose of scheduling refinery oper- ations. This prediction has not come true, however. I know of only one company that has recently started to employ an existing linear scheduling model for the additional purpose of product costing, and this company has no manufacturing plants as complex as an oil refinery, with its many co- products and alternative processes. Generally speaking, cost accountants cannot as yet be considered the main customers of linear programming specialists. It seems useful to list three reasons why the application of scheduling models to costing problems has not become commonplace.

The first reason is insufficient awareness of the fact that the numerical interrelations or constraints in a scheduling model are a sound basis for the reallocation of all types of costs or proceeds, regardless of the question whether or not these costs or proceeds vary linearly with the level or measure of the activity to which they are directly traceable. To elaborate upon this point I refer to the following flow diagrams, representing parts of a production system.

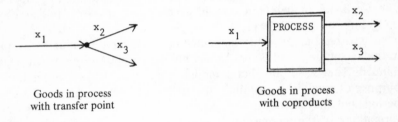

Goods in process
with transfer point

Goods in process
with coproducts

In both cases the units of measure might be chosen to result into the simple material balance equation:

$$x_1 = x_2 + x_3$$

This interrelation between the measures of flow indicates that the measure $x_1$ is uniquely defined by the measures $x_2$ and $x_3$. For this reason the term $c_1 x_1$ in the income function can be replaced by $(c_1 x_2 + c_1 x_3)$, and the costs of the goods in process are thereby distributed over $x_2$ and $x_3$. However, a distribution of values by simple algebraic substitution is not always reason- able. In the examples at hand the reallocation of the costs of $x_1$ is reasonable when the measures of $x_2$ and $x_3$ can be varied independently of each other, so that the measures of both $x_2$ and $x_3$ are needed in order to calculate the measure of $x_1$. This degree of flexibility is implied by the first diagram, but the second one gives no information at all concerning the interrelations. The salient question whether or not objects – such as the measures of $x_2$ and $x_3$ – can be grouped together as independently variable flows of goods, comes into play when equalities in a scheduling model are transformed in the manner that is customary in linear programming. The important point is that, with certain provisos of which I have mentioned only one, all costs directly traceable to $x_1$ might be traced indirectly to $x_2$ and $x_3$ with the aid of a scheduling model. The questions whether or not these costs are variable or fixed, marginal or average, historic or anticipatory, are irrelevant [16, 25, 15, 23, 28].

A second reason why linear programming has found little application in cost accounting is that specialists in model building, like those in related fields, are apt to be over-ambitious. Right from the start they have wanted to build overall corporate models, just like systems analysts before them had advocated total systems studies, and system theorists nowadays dream of an all-embracing system concept. One should have borne in mind that all models are submodels of a larger system, and that subsystems require special criteria in order to appraise situations from an integrated point of view. As I will explain presently, these criteria include things like linking objects, in addition to *flow values* of which a specific type is referred to in the literature as 'shadow prices'. Deeper and more widespread study of the properties of submodels would help to open up a broader field of application for linear models, not only in accounting but also in planning and budgeting [6, 8, 9, 22, 7, 11, 2].

A third reason for little acceptance of linear programming techniques in the accounting field is that model builders are apt to be rather single-minded. They ascertain that a model is mathematically correct for the purpose of establishing optimal levels for the flows of goods in a given period, but they do not always consider the question whether the trans-formations of the income function are consistent with the logic of ac-countancy and econometrics. When interest exists in a breakdown of total optimal income into components that correspond to individual flows of goods or services – and such interest is seldom lacking – it may be advisable to avoid nonzero elements in the right-hand sides of the constraints in the model, by introducing instead a so-called 'bound', i.e. upper and lower limits for individual variables. Furthermore, since values of goods at given points in a production and distribution system are affected by strains at other points, it is essential that not only the upper and lower limits just mentioned, but also the coefficients in the income function, are attached to the variables to which they are directly traceable [5].

## 3.3. MODELS OF THE VALUES AS WELL AS THE MEASURES OF FLOWS

The various points just made are best explained with reference to a simple and precisely defined production system, like the one represented by the following flow diagram.

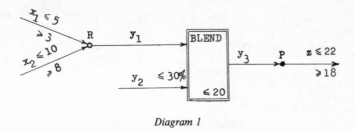

*Diagram 1*

The 2 dots in the diagram, at R and P, are intended to indicate that our exercises with a mathematical model will be concerned not only with the measures of the various flows – which are depicted by arrows – but even more distinctly with the values of the goods flowing past the points R and P in the production system. To put it more explicitly, the dots indicate that our model should include material balance equations for goods flowing to and from these points, with an appropriate 'artificial slack' variable in each equation. Such variables, which will be called $p_o$ and $r_o$ in our example, are the most convenient vehicles by which flow values can be reported in the output of a linear programming exercise. The above diagram shows further that there are 2 sources for the raw material flowing towards point R. The measure of one of these flows has an upper limit of 5 units, and a lower limit of 3 units. Similarly, in the time period under consideration the flow $x_2$ can have a measure between 10 and 8 units. All of the raw material flowing past point R (which is $x_1 + x_2 = y$ units) is blended with another type of raw material, to produce $y_3$ units of an end product. The annotations in the flow diagram imply that $y_1 + y_2 = y_3$, that the availability of $y_2$ is unlimited, that $y_3 = z$, and that the quality of the blended product is acceptable only if $y_2 \leqslant 0.3\,y_3$. The capacity of the blending plant is restricted to 20 units, whereas a marketing demand is expected between 18 and 22 units. Directly traceable costs and proceeds within the relevant ranges are as follows:

$x_1$: variable costs are £1 per unit; fixed costs are £5 in all.
$x_2$: variable costs are £2 per unit; fixed costs are £15 in all.
$y_2$: variable costs are £5 per unit; fixed costs are none.
$y_3$: variable cost of blending is £1 per unit; fixed cost is £55 in all.
$z$: variable proceeds are £10 per unit; fixed costs are £35 in all.

With this information at hand about a given period, let us consider the problem of determining a schedule of flows that maximizes net profit in this period. From an algebraical point of view it would be perfectly correct to formulate this problem in the following manner.

Minimize the income function      $f = -x_1 - 2x_2 - 5y_2 + 9z - 110$

subject to

$$x_1 + x_2 + y_2 = y_3$$
$$y_2 \leqslant .3z$$
$$x_1 + x_2 = y_1$$
$$x_1 + x_2 + y_2 = z$$
$$x_1 + x_2 + y_2 \leqslant 20$$
$$3 \leqslant x_1 \leqslant 5 \qquad 8 \leqslant x_2 \leqslant 10 \qquad 18 \leqslant z \leqslant 22$$

This can be written in a matrix form that is acceptable to a M(athematical) P(rogramming) S(ystem) computer routine, and this matrix does contain material balance equations as prescribed for the points R and P.

| | | $x_1$ | $x_2$ | $y_1$ | $y_2$ | $z$ | RHS |
|---|---|---|---|---|---|---|---|
| LO | | 3 | 8 | | | 18 | |
| UP | | 5 | 10 | | | 22 | |
| N | $-f$ | $-1$ | $-2$ | | $-5$ | 9 | 110 |
| L | $y_3$ | $-1$ | $-1$ | | $-1$ | | |
| L | $s$ | | | | 1 | $-.3$ | |
| E | $r_o$ | $-1$ | $-1$ | 1 | | | |
| E | $p_o$ | $-1$ | $-1$ | | $-1$ | 1 | |
| L | $s_3$ | 1 | 1 | | 1 | | 20 |

Notes: LO = lower limit, UP = upper limit, RHS = right-hand side,
        N = nonconstraining, L = less or equal constraint,
        E = equality.

This initial matrix would produce the following end matrix, which prescribes upper limits (UL) for the flows $x_1$ and $x_2$, because these variables give a positive contribution to the income function. Zero measure is prescribed for the 'individual slack' $s_3$, because its potential contribution is negative. The 'interrelation slack' $s$ has remained absent from the income function during its transformations:

End matrix:

| | | $x_1$ | $x_2$ | $s_3$ | $r_o$ | $p_o$ | RHS |
|---|---|---|---|---|---|---|---|
| | | UL | UL | 0 | — | — | — |
| | $-f$ | 4 | 3 | $-4$ | 0 | $-9$ | 30 |
| | $y_1$ | $-1$ | $-1$ | | 1 | | |
| | $y_2$ | 1 | 1 | 1 | | | 20 |
| | $y_3$ | | | 1 | | | 20 |
| | $z$ | | | 1 | | 1 | 20 |
| | $s$ | $-1$ | $-1$ | $-.7$ | | $.3$ | $-14$ |

The composition of the income function in this end matrix, $f = 4x_1 + 3x_2 - 30$ (apart from zero terms), is perfectly suitable for the conclusion that the corresponding measures of variables ($x_1 = 5$, $x_2 = 10$, and $s_3 = 0$) are optimal; but an accountant would find it hard to swallow that the fixed costs of £110 appear to have drawn a recompense of £80; and the so-called shadow prices at R and P (zero and £9 respectively) have no econometric significance at all. Contiguity with the logic of accountants is achieved by avoiding nonzero elements in the right-hand sides of constraints. Significant shadow prices, more aptly called *flow values*, are obtained by selecting appropriate variables in the initial matrix as bearers of bounding measures and income function coefficients; variables that are situated correctly with respect to the points in the production system where flow values are to be determined. The following formulation is acceptable.

Initial matrix:

| | | LO | 3 | 8 | | | 18 | |
| | | UP | 5 | 10 | | 20 | 22 | |

| | | $x_1$ | $x_2$ | $y_2$ | $y_3$ | $z$ | RHS |
|---|---|---|---|---|---|---|---|
| N | $-f$ | $-1$ | $-2$ | $-5$ | $-1$ | $10$ | $110$ |
| L | $y_1$ | | | $1$ | $-1$ | | |
| L | $s$ | | | $1$ | $-.3$ | | |
| E | $r_0$ | $-1$ | $-1$ | $-1$ | $1$ | | |
| E | $p_0$ | | | | $-1$ | $1$ | |

End matrix:

| | UL | UL | UL | — | — | |

| | $x_1$ | $x_2$ | $y_3$ | $r_0$ | $p_0$ | RHS |
|---|---|---|---|---|---|---|
| $-f$ | $4$ | $3$ | $4$ | $-5$ | $-10$ | $110$ |
| $y_1$ | $-1$ | $-1$ | | $1$ | | |
| $y_2$ | $1$ | $1$ | $-1$ | $-1$ | | |
| $z$ | | | $-1$ | | $1$ | |
| $s$ | $-1$ | $-1$ | $.7$ | $1$ | | |

Apart from zero terms, the initial income function has now been transformed to $f = 4x_1 + 3x_2 + 4y_3 - 110$. This form reflects correctly that the optimal schedule has 3 degrees of freedom, 3 nonzero limiting levels of flow that are independently variable. Furthermore, the flow values that are reported, £5 at point R and £10 at point P are quite meaningful with respect to both aggregate and marginal measures of the products flowing at points R and P. Hence the non-committal term 'flow values'. Their meaning with respect to aggregate measures will be discussed in the next paragraph, in conjunction with the concept of 'linking objects'. In first instance, flow values are marginal values. In our example the material at point R has a marginal value of £5, which means that a relatively small quantity can be withdrawn from the system at a minimum cost of £5 per unit. It so happens that £5 per unit is also the maximum benefit achievable when a relatively small quantity of raw material is inserted into the system at point R. Only in a so-called degenerate situation, with too many constraints, is the insertion value smaller than the extraction value.

## 3.4. LINKING OBJECTS: TRANSFERRERS OF VALUE

When marginal values in a production system are applied as notional transfer prices between separate segments of the system, they cause an equilibrium between the reciprocal supply and demand; this equilibrium has the property that the optimal flow levels of the integral system coincide with flow levels that are optimal for the separate subsystems [4, 17, 3, 13, 18, 30].

This lemma of econometrics has been used for many years as the basis for certain decomposition techniques. Not every model builder realizes, however, that at least some of the subsystems have alternative optimal solutions when they use notional transfer prices. These alternatives are feasible for the subsystem, but infeasible for the integral system. To put it in another way, a notional transfer price – which I call in this paper a 'transfer value' – contains incomplete information for the subsystems concerned. The missing resolving power can be compensated by associating the given transfer value with a particular volume of the internal trade of a specific subsystem, so that the existence of an econometric equilibrium can be verified in this subsystem. This means that a set of $n$ transfer values should be associated with $n$ measures of flow, which I call 'linking objects'. Within the submodels concerned the linking objects are additional 'calculation objects', in the sense that the transfer values should not be considered appropriate links between the subsystems until it has been calculated that the linking 'objects' have zero or 'indifferent' net money value. Such a zero income coefficient of an independently variable transaction of a subsystem reflects the acceptability of alternative levels of the transaction. Without flexibility in the measures of trade between subsystems, in response to variations in the notional transfer price, the whole concept of an equilibrium between supply and demand ceases to exist. The need for flexibility is self-evident when the subsystems are linear, because the supply and demand curves are then in fact step curves.

In order to establish whether or not an equilibrium exists at all the points of transfer between subsystems, it is necessary to determine the optimal *ranges* of supply and demand for specified volumes of goods being exchanged between one subsystem and its associates. The specified volumes are the linking objects. Optimal ranges of supply and demand for one of these objects – at one of the transfer points – are determined under the assumption that the measure of this object can be freely adjusted when marginal changes are made to its notional transfer price, say .01 £/unit upwards and downwards. Further assumptions are that the notional transfer price, and the measure, of linking objects at all other points of transfer between subsystems remain fixed. It follows from this fundamental procedure that the validity of a set of transfer values for a given set of transfer points – validity in the sense that the values cause an equilibrium between supply and demand – can be verified only if each transfer value is associated with a particular linking object. The equilibrium exists with respect to the transactions that are measured by the linking variables. Only as a consequence of *this* equilibrium can it be said that the total supply at each point of transfer is in balance with the total demand. The linking variable itself might represent only part of the supply or part of the demand.

Generally speaking, any structure of transfer values and linking objects is associated with an optimal schedule of activities within a given set of strains. The composition of this set of strains depends on the purpose of the transfer values and linking objects, be it scheduling, costing or recompensing. As we have seen in section 3.3 the transfer values per unit of measure follow directly from an *optimization* routine, provided that the initial matrix is properly formulated. The identification of the corresponding linking objects requires a *post-optimal* procedure, which involves a choice of pivots in the end columns of the relevant artificial material-balance variables. In our example one should identify, in each of the end columns of $r_0$ and $p_0$, a pivot-row variable that measures an inflow or outflow at $R$ and $P$ respectively. The only possible choices are $y_1$ and $z$. The linking objects – for the purpose of scheduling – are therefore ($y_1 = 15$ units) and ($z = 20$ units). Alternative choices are not possible, so that no actual transformations of the end matrix are necessary in this example. In general, however, there may be alternative choices of a linking object to go with a particular transfer value. This means physically that 2 or more items in the material balance must be adjusted in order to extract a marginal quantity from the integral system, at the marginal cost indicated by the transfer value. In such circumstances it is necessary to make post-optimal transformations successively, in order to ensure that the linking objects chosen are compatible with each other. The choice of a specific linking object, out of alternative ones at a given point of transfer, might well reduce the number of choices open at another point of transfer.

Although this short paper cannot cover the various mathematical aspects of linking objects, it is perhaps noteworthy that alternative sets of linking objects – corresponding with the same set of transfer values per unit of measure – are not to be considered a reflection of so-called degenerate solutions. Alternatives might present themselves even when the integral model has no degenerate solution at all. However, if degeneracy does exist, in the sense that a particular linking object has alternative optimal measures in the integral system, the resolving power of the transfer value plus linking object in the subsystem is no longer complete, and must be restored. Otherwise the conclusions drawn from the submodel might correspond with another integral solution than the one to which the linking object corresponds. This is avoided by the identification – in the integral model – of a 'pinning variable', in addition to the linking objects. The pinning variables – flows or interrelation slacks as the case may be – are to be given a minute bonus or penalty in the income function of the subsystem, so that the appropriate end matrix and the conclusions from the submodel are uniquely established.

I used to call linking objects 'key transfers', because the measures and values of these transfers can serve subsystems as keys to the question whether or not particular measurements made within subsystems – like contribution margins, or absorption costs – are valid in the perspective of the integral system. The linking objects of a subsystem act as bearers of the aggregate value that is to be transferred from the subsystem to its various neighbours, for the purpose of the particular measurement in the subsystem. Linking objects are indeed 'transferrers of value', so that each subsystem ends up with a correct perspective of the integral system.

Let me illustrate this point with reference to the problem of scheduling the system of flows described in section 3.3, and portrayed in Diagram 1. There are two approaches to this problem, an integral one and a divisional one.

With the integral approach we use an integral model to answer the question whether or not a specific schedule is optimal. We start from the consideration that the system has 3 degrees of freedom, so that scheduling can be treated as a problem of distributing all variable proceeds and costs over 3 strains, i.e. over 3 objects and/or interrelation slacks, each with a limiting measure that prevents a larger contribution to profit or a smaller drain on profit. Upper limits should correspond with contributions to profit, and lower limits with actual or potential drains on profit. In our example the schedule is optimal if measures of $x_1$, $x_2$ and $y_3$ are at their upper limits, because the integral model shows that these variables acquire positive contribution rates in the profit function (4, 3 and 4 £/unit respectively), when brought into the nonbasis along with the artificial slack variables $r_o$ and $p_o$.

With the divisional approach we use divisional models to answer the question whether or not a particular schedule is optimal for the system as a whole. In our example we might divide the system into 4 subsystems, which we might name after the variables they contain: $(x_1)$, $(x_2)$, $(y_1, y_2, y_3, s)$ and $(z)$. The submodel $(y_1, y_2, y_3, s)$ has 2 degrees of freedom, so that the 4 submodels together have 5 degrees of freedom. This is 2 more than the integral system, because the submodels hang together at 2 points of transfer, by 2 linking objects with fixed measure. The scheduling problem exists of finding these linking objects, each with an aggregate value to be transferred, one object at point $R$ and another at point $P$. How this problem might be solved without the use of a complete integral model, will be discussed in section 3.5. The point at issue is that the transfers of value should result into rates of contribution to profit—for $x_1$, $x_2$ and $y_3$—that are identical to those obtained with the integral approach. That such transfer values do indeed exist, follows from the fact that they can be looked upon as a set of Lagrange's multipliers. The submodels must verify that, for given transfer values of £5 per unit at $R$ and £10 per unit at $P$, and given linking objects ($y_1 = 15$ units) at $R$ and ($z = 20$ units) at $P$, the following conditions hold true:

At point $R$: $x_1 + x_2 = 15$ units,
　　　　　　and the benefit value of $y_1$ is 5 £/unit.

At point $P$: $y_3 = 20$ units,
　　　　　　and the benefit value of $z$ is 10 £/unit.

When this proves to be the case, it can be said that the aggregate benefit value of $y_1$ – consisting of actual cost savings $15 \times £5 = £75$ – is transferred or distributed as follows: a notional revenue of £25 to $x_1$, and £50 to $x_2$. Similarly, an actual revenue of $20 \times £10 = £200$ on $z$ is transferred as a notional revenue to $y_3$. Linking objects transfer their values, and end up with zero or indifferent net value.

The concept of transfer values and linking objects is explained pictorially in Exhibits 1 and 2, which show the flow diagram of a simple oil refinery. It comprises a distiller, a platformer and various blending facilities. The blending of Petrol is subject to a minimum octane number and a maximum vapour pressure. Gasoil blending is subject to a maximum sulphur content, and Fuel oil blending is subject to a maximum viscosity as well as a maximum suphur content. It is assumed that all other quality requirements can be ignored. Applications of crude oils and intermediate products other than the uses indicated in the exhibits are ignored also, on the assumption that such applications are either infeasible or uneconomical. The latter type of assumption, e.g. that the use of Tops as refinery fuel would be uneconomical, is verifiable from the results of a scheduling exercise: intermediate products actually to be used as refinery fuel should prove to have equal flow value, less than that of Tops. The points in the production system where flow values are of interest, have been marked in Exhibit 1, in the same manner as in Diagram 1 (with section 3.3), by noticeable dots. All upper, lower and fixed limits to be taken into account in the scheduling exercise are written into the Exhibits 1 and 2. For convenience they are expressed in identical units of weight per period. The yields and the fuel requirements of the distiller and the platformer are expressed in ratios of weight also. Variable costs of the crude oils used, variable costs of operating the plants, and the variable 'net-backs' from product sales, are not quoted in the exhibits, because the magnitudes of these money values do not affect the principles to be conveyed.

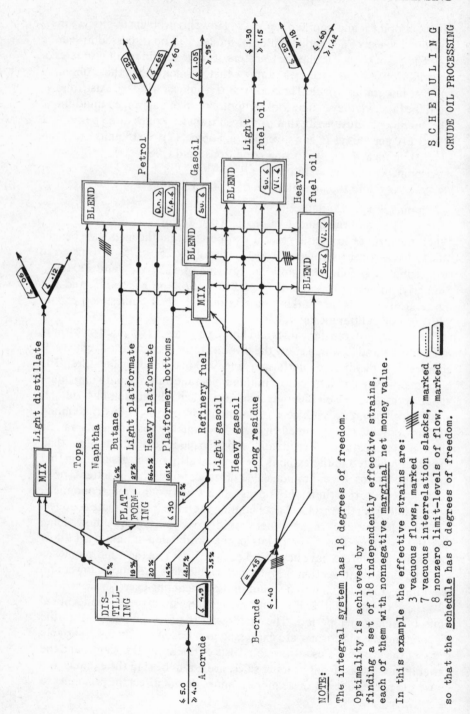

SCHEDULING

CRUDE OIL PROCESSING

NOTE:

The integral system has 18 degrees of freedom.

Optimality is achieved by
finding a set of 18 independently effective strains,
each of them with nonnegative marginal net money value.

In this example the effective strains are:
   3 vacuous flows, marked ————▸
   7 vacuous interrelation slacks, marked ⫽⫽
   8 nonzero limit-levels of flow, marked ⬚
so that the schedule has 8 degrees of freedom.

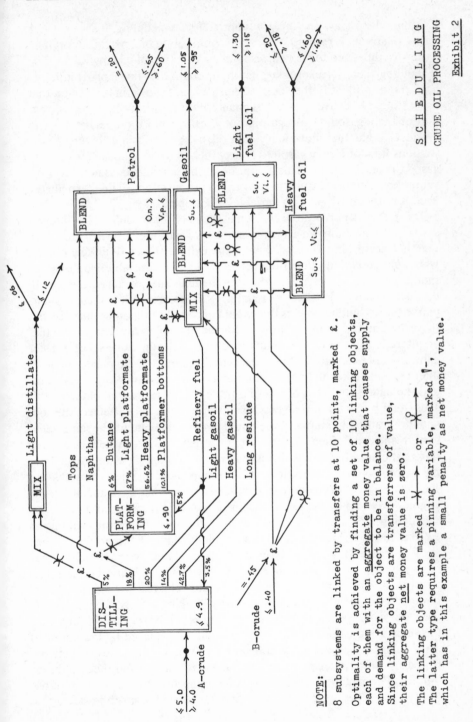

S C H E D U L I N G
CRUDE OIL PROCESSING
Exhibit 2

NOTE:

8 subsystems are linked by transfers at 10 points, marked £.

Optimality is achieved by finding a set of 10 linking objects, each of them with an aggregate money value that causes supply and demand for the object to be in balance.
Since linking objects are transferrers of value, their aggregate net money value is zero.

The linking objects are marked ➤➤ or ➤.
The latter type requires a pinning variable, marked |¬, which has in this example a small penalty as net money value.

Exhibit 1 portrays the integral approach to scheduling. It shows which set of 18 strains is responsible for the composition of a particular optimal basic schedule, and for the corresponding structure of its flow values. The scheduling exercise, an ordinary computer routine for linear programming, has served to identify the set of strains. It is not shown in the exhibit that one of these effective strains has an alternative: by adjusting the distribution of Light gasoil, Heavy gasoil, Long residue and B-crude over the end products Light fuel and Heavy fuel oil, it is permissible to replace the vacuous flow of Heavy gasoil to Heavy fuel oil by a vacuous flow of Light gasoil to Heavy fuel oil. This alteration of the schedule does not affect the values (per unit of measure) of the various product flows. It does explain the need for a socalled 'pinning variable' in Exhibit 2.

This Exhibit 2 portrays the divisional approach to scheduling. The integral system is divided into an arbitrary number of subsystems, which are linked together at 10 points. Accordingly, the exhibit shows 10 linking objects whose measures and values (augmented by 1 pinning variable) would enable the subsystems to determine the subschedules that comprise the overall optimal schedule depicted by Exhibit 1. There are no less than 11 alternative sets of linking objects that would accomplish the same purpose, but these are omitted from the drawing for the sake of clarity. It is evident that an alteration in the choice of linking objects – for the same set of transfer values – does not affect the difference between the aggregate value of internal trade taken in by the nonlinking objects of one of the subsystems, and the aggregate value of internal trade that is transferred out from this subsystem by its linking objects. If this difference were affected, the contribution rates on external trade could not possibly remain the same, identical to those obtained with the integral approach. It is evident also that a different choice of linking objects will result into the same number of linking objects for each of the subsystems, because linking objects must take up the extra degrees of freedom that exist in a subsystem, over and above the degrees taken up by the strains that are effective in the integral approach to scheduling. Consider for instance the subsystem of Petrol blending in Exhibit 2. 6 intermediate products are blended into 1 end product. When the 7 measures of flow are optimal, they are related by 1 material balance equation and 2 effective quality constraints, while the inflow of Naphtha is vacuous, and the outflow of Petrol is .85 units. This leaves 2 degrees of freedom in Petrol blending, to be taken up by 2 linking objects. Exhibit 2 shows the inflows of Light and Heavy platformate as linking objects. According to the underlying calculations, either one can be replaced by the inflow of Tops as linking object, or as transferrer of value. The values being transferred by these objects are benefit values, resulting from the nonlinking inflows. The benefit values of the marketing outflows of Petrol are not transferred. They exceed the sacrifice values of these outflows, so that the contribution rates of these outflows in the income function are positive.

The concept of the transfer of values by linking objects, progressively from one subsystem to the next, is eminently applicable to the problems of costing products and recompensing investments. But before I turn to these subjects, let me introduce the rudiments of a new procedure for the determination – as opposed to the application – of transfer values and linking objects by submodels. It is essentially a decomposition technique for scheduling, but more transparent than most, and more compatible with the desired spread of responsibility in decentralized organizations.

## 3.5. BALANCING PROCEDURES: EVALUATION OF INTRACOMPANY TRADE

A large number of decomposition techniques have been proposed during the past decade, but the current interest in them is largely academic. To my knowledge all of them have proved to be notoriously slow in reaching optimal solutions, and none have been developed in practice into a managerial tool for multinationals, which are by their very nature intent on the adequate spread of responsibilities over their subsidiaries. I have witnessed the application of large refinery scheduling models by Royal Dutch/Shell companies, and the use of certain types of transfer values as input to these models – like 'planning values' and 'differential supply costs' – but the various scheduling models were not designed to test the validity of the transfer values that they used as input, nor the validity of the various flexibilities and constraints that were quoted by the central Service Companies with respect to the volumes of intra-Group trade.

Unfortunately, after decomposition of models was no longer desirable because of relatively small computers being unable to deal with them otherwise, the professional literature has provided little encouragement for actual development of a decomposition technique into procedures of scheduling, costing and recompensing that would be practicable for production companies with widespread activities. Even the terminology of linear programming specialists is discouraging. The simple equations expressing the fact that the quantity of a product flowing towards a point of transfer cannot differ from the quantity flowing away from it, are commonly called 'corporate constraints'. This is then intended to imply that a higher hierarchical level in the organization wishes 'to prevent' the divisions from buying or selling the product of concern in the open market. Decomposition becomes thus a tool for central management, and some commentators conclude that this tool cannot possibly serve as a means to effective decentralization, with adequate subunit autonomy. Subunits suggest alternative levels of trade, and support their suggestions with information that need not always be exhaustive, but – so it is concluded – the decisions originate from a central model at a higher hierarchical level [10, 24, 26, 12, 14, 21].

According to my personal experience these allegations are deceptive. Whatever the hierarchical level where decisions are taken – depending on the type of issues being reviewed – both central and divisional managers would be unworthy of their prerogatives if they failed to work together in discovering yardsticks and bench marks that are relevant to the issues to be decided upon, and understandable to every business man. The discovery of such indicators, like transfer values and linking objects, in an efficient manner that is consistent with the existing degree of decentralization, should be the basic purpose of a decomposition technique. I call such a technique a 'balancing procedure', a name which is more appropriate than the name I used originally: 'bargaining'.

Like most decomposition algorithms the balancing procedure that I propose requires a central model in addition to the submodels. The central model contains interrelations between variables that do not all belong to the same subsystem. To simplify the discussion I shall assume that every one of these interrelations is a material balance equation for a product being transferred between the subsystems. Accordingly, at every stage of the balancing procedure – and there ought to be no more than 1 or 2 stages – the output from the central model exists of nothing else but transfer values with corresponding linking objects and pinning variables, as defined in section 3.4. This is an essential feature of the balancing procedure. The central model is not used for the purpose of enforcing particular sub-schedules. It is used as a central service to divisions, for the purpose of evaluating inter-divisional trade. This economic information is all that needs to be provided by an 'internal trade evaluator' – rather than a 'central coordinator' – as input to the models of subunits. The subunits use their own submodels to check whether or not their subschedules can be fitted together into an integral schedule that is optimal for the combination of submodels.

Another distinguishing feature of a balancing procedure concerns the input provided by the submodels to the central model. This submodel output is made up of heuristic as well as algoristic elements, so that intuitive knowledge and experience of schedulers can be used to full advantage. It is useful to have descriptive names for these various elements before I define the steps in a balancing procedure. Generally speaking, the submodel output consists of some of the rows that make up the end matrix of the sub-model, but suitably condensed by incorporating into the right-hand term all nonbasis terms that correspond neither with a 'transfer variable' nor with a 'mitigating variable'. Transfer variables are those that belong in the inter-divisional material balance equations because they measure the trade between submodels. The mitigating variables in an output row are either 'algoristic' or 'heuristic', depending on the manner in which they are selected. Regardless of the types of mitigating variables taken up in the submodel-output, an output row can be classified as 1. the submodel-part of the 'joint income function', 2. a 'normal relation', 3. an 'algoristic relation', or 4. a 'heuristic relation'. For basis as well as nonbasis variables taken up in the output of a submodel – as input to the central model – the directly traceable upper and lower limits of measure, used as input to the submodel, are reported as input to the central model also. Optimal measures of flow corresponding with the end matrix of a submodel – obtained through the use of intuitive or prescribed notional transfer prices – are excluded from the input to the central model.

The simple production system described in section 3.3 can serve to define the successive steps in a balancing procedure. A casual reader might conclude in the end, that it would have been much simpler to forget about a condensation of submodels in the manner I define, and use instead the complete submodels as input to the central model. It would then be certain that the correct transfer values with corresponding linking and pinning variables are obtained in one go, and the central model employed would be hardly larger than the one obtained in the manner I suggest. This conclusion is invalid, however, when the number of transfer variables in a submodel makes up a relatively small proportion of the total number of submodel variables. The procedure I suggest comes into its own, when the submodels are too large to be amalgamated conveniently, whereas the total number of transfer variables is relatively small. In such cases a well conducted balancing procedure along the lines I suggest, resulting into a reasonably small central model, might yet produce the appropriate transfer values plus linking and pinning variables in one go. The submodels that I have experimented with have not been large enough to prove the opposite.

Let us thus turn to the numerical data given in section 3.3 with the scheduling problem of Diagram 1. The divisional approach to this problem, as discussed in section 3.4, involved 4 subsystems, but in order to allow certain aspects of the balancing procedure to come out more clearly, I shall now consider only 3 subsystems by combining the variables $x_1$ and $x_2$, together with a new variable $x_3$, into one subsystem. This leads to the flow diagrams shown in Diagrams 2a, 2b and 2c.

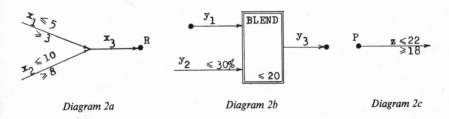

Diagram 2a                         Diagram 2b                         Diagram 2c

The initial matrices of the corresponding submodels are shown below. The 'transfer variables' are $x_3$, $y_1$, $y_3$ and $z$. The variable $f$ in each of the submodels represents the submodel-part of the 'joint income function'; the constant terms in these functions are ignored. $f_a$, $f_b$ and $f_c$ are the income functions to be used for submodel optimization; they include the transfer values $v$ and $w$ – at the transfer points $R$ and $P$ respectively – which are to be determined by the balancing procedure.

Initial matrices of submodels:

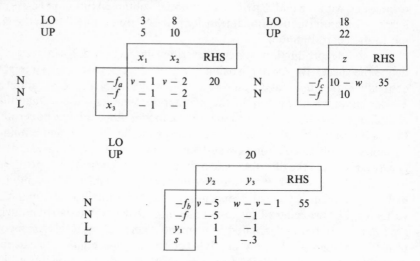

The balancing procedure begins with submodel optimizations. The controllers of the submodels estimate, independently of each other and chiefly by wishful guesswork, which of the variables in their submodel are likely to show up in the nonbasis of the end matrix. The guesswork should be guided by past experience as to the relative levels of the transfer values and the likelihood that particular transfer variables will eventually be discovered as linking objects. In our example let us assume that each controller hopes for maximum turnover or throughput, while none of them expects to be landed with a linking object. The supply controller chooses to begin with $v = 3$ £/unit, the distribution controller chooses $w = 9$ £/unit, and the processing controller $v = 4$ and $w = 7$. These wishful assumptions result into the following end matrices.

End matrices of submodels:

|  | UL | UL |  |
|---|---|---|---|
|  | $x_1$ | $x_2$ | RHS |
| $-f_a$ | 2 | 1 | 20 |
| $-f$ | −1 | −2 |  |
| $x_3$ | −1 | −1 |  |

|  | UL |  |
|---|---|---|
|  | $z$ | RHS |
| $-f_c$ | 1 | 35 |
| $-f$ | 10 |  |

|        |        | 0   | UL  |     |
|--------|--------|-----|-----|-----|
|        |        | $y_2$ | $y_3$ | RHS |
| $-f_b$ |        | $-1$ | $2$ | $55$ |
| $-f$   |        | $-5$ | $-1$ |     |
| $y_1$  |        | $1$  | $-1$ |     |
| $s$    |        | $1$  | $-.3$ |     |

At this point of the procedure it is noted by the controller of the processing model, that the transfer variable $y_3$ has ended in the nonbasis. For this reason he should reconsider the implication that $y_3$ gives a positive contribution to the submodel income function $f_b$. It might be equally reasonable to assume that $y_3$ will become 'linking object' in the end, with a prescribed measure somewhat below 20 units, and with zero contribution to the submodel income function. When such assumptions are indeed equally reasonable, it is desirable to reoptimize with a fixed measure and an amended transfer value (e.g. in this example $y_3 = 18$ and $w = 5$), before the submodel is subjected to further postoptimal procedures. This would leave less scope for condensation of the submodel, but might enhance the convergence to the overall optimum (speaking generally). We shall assume that $w$, and the limiting measure of $y_3$, are not amended by the processing controller. We shall further assume that the distribution controller, who has noticed that the transfer variable $z$ has ended in the nonbasis, will not amend $w$ nor the limiting measure of $z$ in the distribution submodel.

It must now be decided which rows in the end matrices of the submodels should serve as input to the central model, and to what extent these rows might be condensed. I shall discuss the 3 submodels jointly, although in fact each of them is considered on its own merits. The first rows to be selected, in addition to row $f$, are the *'normal relations'*. These are the rows with a transfer variable as basis variable; rows $x_3$ and $y_1$ in our example. The first elements to be selected in these rows – as eventual input to the central model – are those corresponding with transfer variables in the nonbasis; in our example element $(y_1, y_3)$ only. Now if all the remaining elements in rows $x_3$ and $y_1$ were incorporated into the RHS, these rows would reduce to $x_3 = 15$ and $y_1 - y_3 = 0$; but these stringent relations should be softened by the choice of *'mitigating variables'*, both in the rows $x_3$ and $y_1$ themselves, and in other rows to be selected as input to the central model. No matrix elements are incorporated into the RHS until the selection of rows has been completed, and corresponding mitigating columns have been safeguarded or exempted from inclusion in the RHS.

The first mitigating variables – 'algoristic' ones – are chosen as follows. One gives a fixed bound to all transfer variables that have ended in the nonbasis. In our rather trivial example one need not give further consideration to the distribution submodel (because this submodel lacks variables other than the transfer variable $z$), but one should fix the measure of the NB (nonbasis) transfer variable $y_3$ at 20. Next one analyzes the effect of variations to the transfer value of BS (basis) transfer variables. In the terminology of M(athematical) P(rogramming) S(ystem): what are the 'limiting processes'? Which variables are the first to move from NB to BS, when the transfer value of a BS transfer variable is changed upwards and downwards? These are accepted as 'algoristic mitigating variables'. By analyzing changes in the value of $x_3$, one comes to accept $x_2$ as a mitigating variable; and by analyzing changes in the value of $y_1$, one comes to accept $y_2$ as a mitigating variable.

While such mitigating variables are selected, one should investigate also whether BS transfer variables in the submodels have alternative optimal measures. They have not in our example, but when they do have them it should be investigated, which other BS variables – other than transfer variables – acquire an alternative optimal measure along with the BS transfer variable of concern. The rows corresponding with these other BS variables are accepted as '*algoristic relations*'. They are accepted as input to the central model along with the 'normal relations', and may give rise to the choice of additional mitigating variables of the algoristic type.

'*Heuristic relations*' are next to be added. These are relations – in the end matrix of a submodel – whose BS variable might conceivably prove to have a limiting measure (or bound) that is optimal for the combination of submodels, according to previous experience. Such relations give rise again to additional mitigating variables of the algoristic type. Mitigating *columns* of the *heuristic* type are to be added in conclusion. They correspond with a NB variable – in the end matrix of a submodel – whose limiting measure might conceivably prove to be nonoptimal for the combination of submodels.

Having thus completed the identification of submodel rows and columns that are desired as input to the central model, the remaining rows are ignored, and the remaining columns are incorporated into the RHS at their suboptimal levels. In our example row $s$ is ignored, and column $x_1$ is moved to the RHS. The submodels are thus condensed as follows.

Condensed end matrices of submodels:

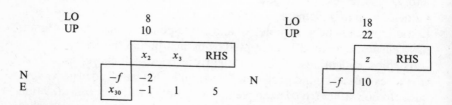

|  | $y_1$ | $y_2$ | $y_3$ | RHS |
|---|---|---|---|---|
| LO |  |  |  |  |
| UP |  |  | 20 |  |
| N   $-f$ |  | $-5$ | $-1$ |  |
| E   $y_{10}$ | 1 | 1 | $-1$ |  |

In general, artificial variables like $x_{30}$ and $y_{10}$ are introduced for all BS transfer variables, and for all nontransfer BS variables with a limiting measure other than a lower bound zero. The condensed end matrices can then be added to the interdivisional material balance equations. The central model thus obtained has nonzero elements in the right hand side – e.g. element $(x_{30}, \text{RHS})$ – but these do not cause any confusion, because the composition of the combined income function is irrelevant: The central model serves only to determine the levels of the transfer values, and to identify the corresponding linking and pinning variables. This is done as if the condensed central model were a complete integral model, in the manner described in section 3.4.

Initial matrix of central model:

|  | $x_3$ | $y_1$ | $y_3$ | $z$ | $x_2$ | $y_2$ | RHS |
|---|---|---|---|---|---|---|---|
| LO |  |  |  |  | 18 | 8 |  |
| UP |  |  | 20 | 22 | 10 |  |  |
| $-f$ |  |  | $-1$ | 10 | $-2$ | $-5$ |  |
| E  $r_0$ | $-1$ | 1 |  |  |  |  |  |
| E  $p_0$ |  |  | $-1$ | 1 |  |  |  |
| E  $x_{30}$ | 1 |  |  |  | $-1$ |  | 5 |
| E  $y_{10}$ |  | 1 | $-1$ |  |  | 1 |  |

End matrix of central model, in which irrelevant artificials are omitted:

|  | $x_2$ | $y_3$ | $r_0$ | $p_0$ | RHS |
|---|---|---|---|---|---|
|  | UL | UL | – | – |  |
| $-f$ | 3 | 4 | $-5$ | $-10$ | $-25$ |
| $x_3$ | $-1$ |  |  |  | 5 |
| $y_1$ | $-1$ |  | 1 |  | 5 |
| $y_2$ | 1 | $-1$ | $-1$ |  | $-5$ |
| $z$ |  | $-1$ |  | 1 |  |

Postoptimal end matrix of central model, after the linking objects are identified:

|        | $x_2$ | $y_3$ | $y_1$ | $z$ | RHS |
|--------|-------|-------|-------|-----|-----|
| $-f$   | $-2$  | $-6$  | $5$   | $10$ |     |
| $x_3$  | $-1$  |       |       |     | $5$ |
| $r_o$  | $-1$  |       | $1$   |     | $5$ |
| $y_2$  |       | $-1$  | $1$   |     |     |
| $p_o$  |       | $-1$  |       | $1$ |     |

The relevant data concerning transfer values, linking objects and pinning variables are passed on to the controllers of the submodels, and the central model is then scrapped except for its interdivisional material balance equations, which might yet be needed in a second round of balancing. With the information obtained the submodels are optimized, and it is up to the controllers of submodels with linking and pinning variables, to verify whether or not all schedules thus obtained are optimal for the combination of subsystems. Linking and pinning objects should have an indifferent net money value within the subsystem, and the interdivisional supply and demand for linking objects should prove to be in balance. In our example the controller of the processing model should affirm that the linking object $y_1$ has a zero coefficient in row $f_b$ of the end matrix, and that the suboptimal measure of $x_3$ (supply model) equals that of $y_1$. Similarly, the controller of the distribution model should affirm that the linking object $z$ has a zero coefficient in row $f_c$ of the end matrix, and that the suboptimal measure of $y_3$ (processing model) equals $z$.

I shall not go into the academic question whether or not the balancing procedure I have just described would converge to an optimum, if heuristic rows and columns in the central model were ignored. A much more important question is whether or not the partly heuristic procedure would converge in one go or two, under practical conditions, with large submodels and a relatively small number of interdivisional transfer points. I have not (yet) been able to build up experience in this matter. An important requirement is that the submodels are formulated in a manner that is compatible with orthodox concepts on the transfer of value from one object progressively to other objects. This is important particularly when balancing procedures are applied to exercises in costing and recompensing, as opposed to scheduling. In the former types of exercises the question of convergence to an optimum does not even arise. A schedule exists already, and it is merely a question of transferring values progressively to end products, or to variables associated with investments, instead of variables that happen to be subject to short-run strains.

## 3.6. DEGREES OF FREEDOM AND CHANNELS OF VALUATION

Costing and recompensing exercises have in common that they are done for a given schedule of activities. The measures of flow that comprise the schedule may be retrospective or anticipatory. In either case they correspond with a set of strains during the relatively short interval of time to which the schedule corresponds. When the time interval lies wholly or partly in the future, the scheduled measures of flow are calculated from the strains that are expected to be effective. Conversely, when the schedule consists of historic measures of flow, a set of effective strains can be reconstructed from the recorded flows. Recorded as well as planned schedules are associable with a set of effective strains, i.e. active upper and lower limits of flow, and/or vacuous interrelation slacks.

In an algebraic sense – although perhaps not in a practical sense – these bounding measures of flows and slacks are independently variable, and their number corresponds with the degrees of freedom of the production system. This number might not be the same for successive intervals of time, but it is known or can be reconstructed for any given production schedule, along with a set of independent interrelations, which can serve to determine the measures of all flows and interrelation slacks not affected by their own individual bounds. This set of independent interrelations constitutes the only logical basis for reallocation of directly traceable costs and proceeds to the effective strains, in a process of scheduling.

A basis for costing, or for recompensing, must be found by transformations of this set of independent interrelations (and by possible additions as discussed in section 3.7). Thus when products are to be costed, the measures of flow of these products should be fixed in the nonbasis as notional strains. This exchange of variables between basis and nonbasis is not completely free, however, and the resulting product costs may turn out to be invalid even when the exchanges of variables between basis and nonbasis appear to be appropriate to begin with.

Let us consider for instance the search for a costing basis for the crude oil processing schedule of Exhibit 1. This schedule corresponds to a system with 18 degrees of freedom, evidenced by 18 variables in the final nonbasis, in addition to the various artificial slack variables with a fixed zero measure. Exhibit 1 shows that 10 of these 18 NB (nonbasis) variables have a zero measure; nonzero measures are feasible but would reduce the overall income function. 3 of these variables are vacuous flows, and the other 7 are vacuous interrelation slacks corresponding to quality constraints. The 3 vacuous flows in the NB might be scrapped; none of them should be exchanged with the BS (basis) flow of Light fuel oil, even if a pivot element is available, because the costs of end products must be associated with actual expense, not with the potential costs of vacuous flows.

The vacuous interrelation slacks in the nonbasis – of which there are 7 in Exhibit 1 – might be scrapped also, as a rule, because an exchange with a BS flow of an end product would imply the absence of economic reasons why the schedule calls for end products of minimum quality. By exception, however, when products of better than minimum quality are indeed produced in accounting periods adjacent to the one of concern, it may be desirable to ignore the quality constraint, by moving the corresponding vacuous interrelation slack to the basis. This change gives the schedule an extra degree of freedom; the costing basis would be 'degenerate', and product costs would be influenced by something nonexistent, i.e. flexible product quality. The influence would be indirect, however, because the basis variable with zero measure is an algebraic slack, so that no potential costs nor proceeds are directly traceable to it. For this reason I consider the degeneracy of the costing basis acceptable, provided it results in identical costing structures for successive periods of accounting.

In the example of Exhibit 1 we shall disallow a degenerate costing basis. This leaves the schedule with 8 degrees of freedom, i.e. 8 nonvacuous flows that can serve as calculation objects or recipients of money values. It so happens that 8 is also the number of outflows of the 5 end products. We might thus be tempted to conclude that a good costing basis is obtained by moving the inflow of B-crude and the throughflow of the distiller from the NB to the BS, in exchange for outflows of Light and Heavy fuel oil.

Exhibit 3 illustrates the results obtained in this manner. The two post-optimal transformations result into an end matrix that can be obtained by renewed optimization. Fixed measures must then be prescribed for variables that are to end in the nonbasis, and the bounds on the inflow of B-crude and the throughflow of the distiller should be scrapped in order to avoid degenerate conditions and possible rounding errors. The measures of all BS variables in the newly obtained end matrix will prove to be identical to those that are optimal in the short-run – according to the scheduling exercise – and these measures are uniquely defined by the 8 quantities of end products made. Accordingly, the end products absorb all sacrifices of consumable and durable producer goods, in proportions that are algebraically correct. These proportions are not influenced by the magnitudes and types of sacrifices that we wish to consider directly traceable to particular flows of materials. Nevertheless the resultant product costs, associated with the structure of linking objects or 'value transferrers' shown in Exhibit 3, are invalid.

The reason is that classic concepts of costing call for a 'viable' system of activities, i.e. a complete system that covers successively the acquisition of one or more raw materials, and the entailing activities, including the disposal of one or more end products. Value is added to raw material, and thereafter to goods in process, until corresponding end products are

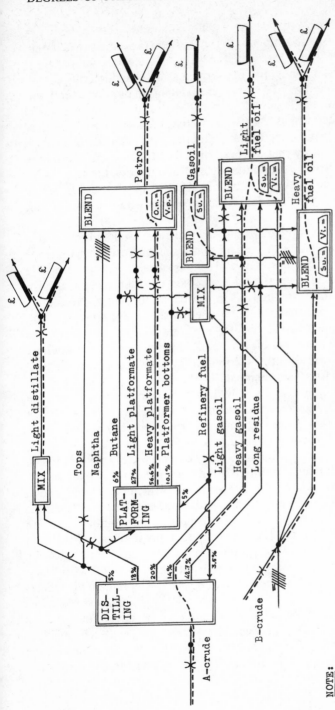

TRIAL COSTING SCHEME
FOR OIL PRODUCTS
Exhibit 3

NOTE:

8 degrees of freedom are taken up by choosing 5 "main" products.
A resultant set of 17 linking objects is marked

Alternative sets can be chosen with objects marked

2 of the proposed main products prove to lack a complete
costing channel, along linking objects back to an item of
raw material.    The costing channels are marked

In view of the lack of at least 1 complete channel per product,
the proposed costing scheme is incompatible with the schedule.

disposed of in the market place. An equally complete system of activities is required in order to recompense the investments that make the system of activities feasible. For this reason it must be possible to discover 'valuation channels' in a flow diagram, converging at a calculation object, and running back to an inflow of raw material and/or an outflow of end product. Thus in Exhibit 3 it should be possible to draw 'costing channels' from the end products across transfer points to value transferrers or linking objects, all the way back to the raw material used; and these channels should have the property that a rise of directly traceable costs anywhere along the channel would result into higher product costs. I postulate that at least one complete costing channel should exist for the outflow of end products chosen as 'main products', i.e. products whose costs per unit are to be determined.

Exhibit 3 shows a complete costing channel for Gasoil and for the two Fuel oils. It may be noted in passing that a second costing channel for Light fuel oil, back to B-crude, is invalid because a rise of directly traceable costs of B-crude would lower the calculated costs of Light fuel oil, according to the column of Light fuel oil in the trial end matrix. No costing channel exists for Light distillate, nor for Petrol; the dashed lines in Exhibit 3 cannot be continued to the distiller — across the next transfer points upstream — because the flows of Tops and Naphtha from the distiller are nonlinking objects. Moreover, the columns for Light distillate and Petrol in the trial end matrix lack elements in the rows for A-crude and the distiller. These are the reasons why I call the combination of 5 main products *incompatible* with the production schedule.

This incompatibility results essentially from insufficient degrees of freedom, not in the production schedule as a whole, but in the subschedule of distilling. The distilling process has only one degree of freedom, which is taken up by one linking object in Exhibit 3: the measure of Heavy gasoil. As a consequence there is no distiller outflow by which raw material costs can be transferred onwards to Petrol and Light distillate, so that these end products cannot be considered main products in combination with Gasoil and the two Fuel oils. It is necessary to apply the classic distinction between main products and by-products. End products whose costs one wishes to compare are chosen as main products. The outflows of these products are chosen as '*main calculation objects*'. The remaining degrees of freedom must be taken up in the nonbasis by provisional recipients of values, which I call '*ancillary calculation objects*', and which give rise to '*ancillary interrelations*' between measures of flow. Such ancillary interrelations embody criteria for the distribution of values, in addition to the criteria that apply in scheduling because of technical relations between measures of flow.

## 3.7. ANCILLARY INTERRELATIONS IN COSTING AND RECOMPENSING

Ancillary interrelations are made necessary by degrees of freedom that exceed the number of main calculation objects in a given schedule. In first instance the extra degrees of freedom find their expression in ancillary calculation objects with fixed bounds in the nonbasis. These objects cannot be chosen arbitrarily, however, and it may be necessary to choose some of them by trial and error when the production system is very complex. Each ancillary calculation object must satisfy the condition that ordinary accounting logic can be applied for the purpose of replacing the fixed bound of the object by an ancillary interrelation, i.e. an equation that expresses the measure of the ancillary object in those of other objects. Moreover, each equation thus added to the matrix must be independent of all other relations between measures of flow.

Accounting logic requires that values are passed on progressively from one flow to adjacent ones. For this reason the measure of an ancillary calculation object should be related to those of other flows separated from it by only one transfer point or by none at all. The interrelation to be formulated should thus be applicable to a small subsystem, cut out from the integral system (by means of transfer values and linking objects). Let us consider some examples of subsystems that can serve to formulate ancillary interrelations in valuation exercises.

There are two distinct types of ancillary calculation objects, which I call '*external*' and '*internal*'. The former type serves to amend the average value passed onwards by a parallel flow. The flows $x_1$ in the Diagrams 3a to 3d, with a scheduled measure of $x_1^*$, are examples of external ancillary objects

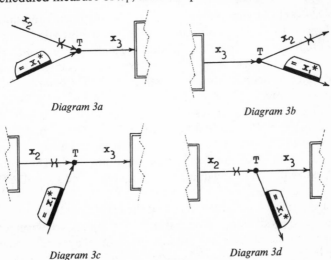

Diagram 3a                    Diagram 3b

Diagram 3c                    Diagram 3d

in a costing exercise: an additional inflow of raw material in Diagram 3a, an additional outflow of a by-product in Diagram 3b, a net reduction of stock during the accounting period in Diagram 3c, and a net increase of stock in Diagram 3d. The last flow would be main calculation object when the costing exercise deals with inventorial items of costs; the increase of a stock level is ancillary calculation object, however, in a (separate) costing exercise dealing with production costs that for one reason or another are to be omitted from the sacrifice value of inventories.

In each of the examples given the diagram shows $x_2^*$ as the linking object, i.e. as the transferrer of value at point $T$. Thus the variable $x_2$ is situated in the basis of the costing model, but its flow must be 'clamped down' to a magnitude $x_2^*$ if the integral system were cut at point $T$. The flow of $x_1$ is 'weighted down' in the diagrams to $x_1 = x_1^*$. Accounting logic requires that $x_3^*$ receives not only the aggregate value of $x_2^*$ but also of $x_1^*$. This means in Diagrams 3a, 3b and 3c that the joint value of $x_2^*$ and $x_1^*$ must be passed across point $T$ to $x_3^*$; and this is achieved by adding the following equation to the model:

$$x_1 = \frac{x_1^*}{x_2^*} x_2$$

In Diagram 3d the aggregate value of $x_1^*$ would have to be passed directly to $x_3^*$, without crossing point $T$; and this is done by the equation:

$$x_1 = \frac{x_1^*}{x_3^*} x_3$$

Ancillary objects of the *internal* type are more difficult to choose than external ones. The criteria used must make it possible to deal with them in a manner that fits in with ordinary accounting logic. I have included in these criteria the requirement that the ancillary object serves to make up a material balance between two successive flows in a complete valuation channel, a channel that runs all the way from a raw material to an end product. Two typical examples of internal ancillary objects are shown in Diagrams 4a and 4b. In both of them the ancillary object called $x_1$, 'weighted down' at the scheduled measure $x_1 = x_1^*$, belongs in a material balance equation that can be written for point $R$. In Diagram 4a the two successive flows in the valuation channel are $x_2$ and $x_5$, and in Diagram 4b these are $x_0$ and $x_5$.

For ease of discussion we suppose that the main calculation objects to be valued are end products to be costed. Linking objects – determined by the usual post-optimal procedure – are marked in the diagrams whenever they are situated within the part of the integral production system depicted by these diagrams. The first question is now, where the dashed costing channel

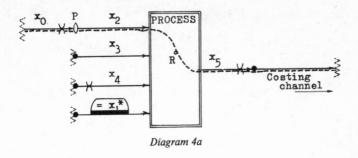

*Diagram 4a*

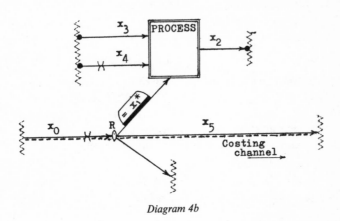

*Diagram 4b*

should be cut for the purpose of extracting – from the integral system – a subsystem around the ancillary object $x_1^*$. This question is answered by looking at the end column of $x_1$. Let us suppose that this column has a nonzero element for the linking object $x_0$ in the costing channel (perhaps accompanied by nonzero elements for the upstream objects), whereas matrix elements are lacking for the linking objects further downstream along the costing channel. The costing channel must then be cut immediately after $x_0$, at point $P$ in Diagram 4a, and at point $R$ in Diagram 4b. The reasoning is that the linking objects further downstream cannot pass onwards correct values unless the values absorbed by $x_1^*$ are first distributed over other objects. These other objects must be found in a subsystem around $x_1$, which can now be extracted from the integral system in a straightforward manner. Apart from interrelation slacks pertaining to the processes depicted, the subsystem contains the flows $(x_1, x_2, x_3, x_4, x_5)$ in Diagram 4a, and the flows $(x_1, x_2, x_3, x_4)$ in Diagram 4b. In both cases the end column $x_1$ in the submodel, after separation from the integral model, has the following composition:

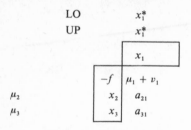

$\mu_1$, $\mu_2$ and $\mu_3$ are the directly traceable values of $x_1$, $x_2$ and $x_3$ in the income function of the submodel, thus including the transfer values. $v_1$ is the indirectly traceable value of $x_1$; it is given by the equality:

$$v_1 = -a_{21}\mu_2 - a_{31}\mu_3$$

I reason now as follows. $x_1$ is an independently variable flow, whose measure $x_1^*$ collects costs, which amount to $(-x_1^*\mu_1)$ money units. These costs are offset by savings collected by $x_1^*$ from the 'contributory' flows $x_2$ and $x_3$. These savings amount to $(-x_1^*a_{21}\mu_2)$ and $(-x_1^*a_{31}\mu_3)$ money units respectively, which adds up to $(x_1^*v_1)$ money units. It is thus reasonable to distribute net value of $x_1$ over the contributory flows $x_2$ and $x_3$ in the proportions:

$$\frac{-a_{21}\mu_2}{v_1} \quad \text{and} \quad \frac{-a_{31}\mu_3}{v_1}.$$

This is achieved by adding the following ancillary interrelation to the overall costing model:

$$x_1 = \frac{-a_{21}\mu_2}{v_1} \cdot \frac{x_1^*}{x_2^*} \cdot x_2 + \frac{-a_{31}\mu_3}{v_1} \cdot \frac{x_1^*}{x_3^*} \cdot x_3$$

This equation replaces the fixed bound on $x_1$, provided that it is an independent equation. If it is not, the submodel must be enlarged, or a different ancillary calculation object must be chosen. After an ancillary calculation object has been replaced by an independent equation, the submodel around the object must be reincorporated into the integral model, so that other internal ancillary objects further down the costing channel can be attended to, and/or product costs are determined.

Internal ancillary objects, like by-products, are necessary evils. It is desirable to choose objects with small measure, as far as possible down the costing channel to the 'most important' main product. In this manner these objects are likely to cause the least distortion to an otherwise straightforward valuation structure, although experience shows that alternative choices of ancillary calculation objects result quite often in identical values for the main calculation objects. This is most evidently the case when there is clearly a causal relationship between specific sacrifices of producer goods and a particular volume of an end product.

A few examples of valuation are in order. To begin with let us consider the calculation of product costs for the simple production system described in section 3.3 with Diagram 1. Our scheduling exercise produced an end matrix with 3 nonvacuous flows in the nonbasis, $x_1 = 5$, $x_2 = 10$, and $y_3 = 20$. There is only 1 end product, however, with an outflow $z = 20$. Accordingly we need 2 ancillary calculation objects. The flow $x_1 = 5$ presents itself as external ancillary object, and we try $y_2 = 5$ as internal ancillary object. This produces the following results.

Trial costing matrix:

| $c$ | | 10 | −1 | −5 | | | |
|---|---|---|---|---|---|---|---|
| | FX BND | 20 | 5 | 5 | | | |
| | | $z$ | $x_1$ | $y_2$ | $r_0$ | $p_0$ | RHS |
| | $-f$ | 7 | 1 | −3 | −2 | −3 | 110 |
| −2 | $x_2$ | −1 | 1 | 1 | ⊝1 | −1 | |
| | $y_1$ | −1 | | 1 | | −1 | |
| −1 | $y_3$ | −1 | | | | ⊝1 | |
| | $s$ | −.3 | | 1 | | −.3 | |

FX BND = fixed nonzero limits for NB variables.
c      = variable costs and proceeds of BS and NB variables.
f      = transformed income function (with transformed coefficients c).
◯      = pivots identifying linking objects on costing channel.

Corresponding flow diagram:

with effective strains marked
    main calculation object marked
    external ancillary object marked
    internal ancillary object marked

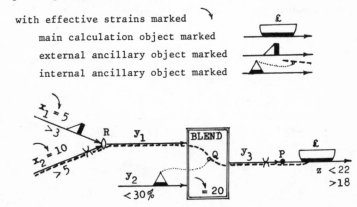

*Diagram 5*

We observe that all 3 flows $y_3$, $y_1$ and $x_2$ along the dotted line have negative elements in column $z$, so that a rise in costs of any of them would cause higher costs of $z$. We observe further that linking objects exist for the transfer of costs along the dotted line at the transfer points $R$ and $P$. The line $(x_2, y_1, y_3)$ can be accepted therefore as costing channel of $z$.

$x_1$ qualifies as external ancillary object, because it is an inflow of material additional to $x_2$. The cost of $x_1$ might be passed on jointly with the cost of $x_2$, so that the flow value at point $R$ reflects average raw material costs. This can be achieved by adding the equation $x_1 = 0.5\,x_2$.

$y_2$ qualifies as internal ancillary object, because it belongs in a material balance equation with 2 successive objects, $y_1$ and $y_3$, of the costing channel. Moreover, the end column of $y_2$ lacks an element pertaining to a flow that can serve as an alternative ancillary object, contributing to a material balance at a point downwards from point $Q$ on the costing channel.

Thus we accept the trial costing matrix as suitable for the costing exercise (unless we should discover later on that no independent interrelations can be formulated for the ancillary objects we have chosen).

We continue this exercise by attending to the external ancillary object. Adding interrelation $x_1 = 0.5\,x_2$ gives with the aid of an artificial slack variable $x_{20}$:

|        | $z$  | $x_1$ | $y_2$ | $r_0$ | $p_0$ | RHS |
|--------|------|-------|-------|-------|-------|-----|
| $-f$   | 7    | 1     | $-3$  | $-2$  | $-3$  | 110 |
| $x_2$  | $-1$ | 1     | 1     | $-1$  | $-1$  |     |
| $y_1$  | $-1$ |       | 1     |       | $-1$  |     |
| $y_3$  | $-1$ |       |       |       | $-1$  |     |
| $s$    | $-.3$|       | 1     |       | $-.3$ |     |
| $x_{20}$ | $-.5$ | 1.5 | .5    | $-.5$ | $-.5$ |     |

After transformation and omission of column $x_{20}$, we find:

| $c$ |  |  | 10 | $-5$ |  |  |
|-----|--|--|----|------|--|--|

| FX BND |  |  | 20 | 5 |  |  |
|--------|--|--|----|---|--|--|

|      |          | $z$    | $y_2$   | $r_0$    | $p_0$    | RHS |
|------|----------|--------|---------|----------|----------|-----|
|      | $-f$     | 7.333  | $-3.333$| $-1.667$ | $-2.667$ | 110 |
| $-2$ | $x_2$    | $-.667$| .667    | $-.667$  | $-.667$  |     |
|      | $y_1$    | $-1$   | 1       |          | $-1$     |     |
| $-1$ | $y_3$    | $-1$   |         |          | $-1$     |     |
|      | $s$      | $-.3$  | 1       |          | $-.3$    |     |
| $-1$ | $x_1$    | $-.333$| .333    | $-.333$  | $-.333$  |     |

We attend now to the internal ancillary object $y_2$ by cutting the production flows at points $R$ and $P$. The end matrix is transformed by bringing the artificial slacks $r_0$ and $p_0$ into the basis, in exchange for the linking objects.

| | | | | | | |
|---|---|---|---|---|---|---|
| $c$ | | | 10 | −5 | −2 | −1 |
| | FX BND | 20 | 5 | | | |
| | | $z$ | $y_2$ | $x_2$ | $y_3$ | RHS |
| | $-f$ | 10 | −5 | −2.5 | −1 | 110 |
| $(t_r = 1.667)$ | $r_0$ | | −1 | −1.5 | 1 | |
| | $y_1$ | | | 1 | −1 | |
| $(t_p = 2.667)$ | $p_0$ | 1 | | | −1 | |
| | $s$ | | | 1 | −.3 | |
| −1 | $x_1$ | | | | −.5 | |

The equalities $r_0$ and $p_0$ in this end matrix are eliminated by incorporating the transfer values $t_r$ and $t_p$ into the final income function. The unadulterated material balances at $R$ and $P$ are used in a similar manner for the purpose of incorporating the transfer values into the initial income function, with coefficients $\mu$ (instead of $c$). This produces the following end matrix for the cut-up production system.

| | | | | | | |
|---|---|---|---|---|---|---|
| $\mu$ | | | 7.333 | −5 | −.333 | 1.667 |
| | FX BND | 20 | 5 | 10 | 20 | |
| | | $z$ | $y_2$ | $x_2$ | $y_3$ | RHS |
| | $-f$ | 7.333 | −3.333 | 0 | 0 | 110 |
| −1.667 | $y_1$ | | 1 | | −1 | |
| | $s$ | | 1 | | −.3 | |
| .667 | $x_1$ | | | −.5 | | |

A separate submodel around the internal ancillary object $y_2$ can be completed by omitting irrelevant columns and superfluous elements in row $f$. Moreover, the term in the right hand side of row $f$ should be amended to show fixed costs within the submodel as quoted in section 3.3.

| | | | | |
|---|---|---|---|---|
| $\mu$ | | −5 | 1.667 | |
| | FX BND | 5 | 20 | |
| | | $y_2$ | $y_3$ | RHS |
| | $-f$ | | | 55 |
| −1.667 | $y_1$ | 1 | −1 | |
| | $s$ | 1 | −.3 | |

$\Rightarrow y_1^* = 15$

According to the general procedure for internal ancillary objects, it can now be worked out that the fixed bound of $y_2$ in the integral costing model should be replaced by the ancillary interrelation $y_2 = 0.333\ y_1$. To put it simply, and in terms that in this elementary example are self-evident from the start: economic consumption of producer goods makes it necessary to use 3 times as much $y_1$ as $y_2$, and the product costs of $z$ should be calculated accordingly.

Thus we obtain the following final costing matrix. Not only is the equation $y_2 = 0.333\ y_1$ added, but the constant costs of 110 in the right hand side of the income function have been distributed over the coefficients $c$, in accordance with the data given in section 3.3. This has produced the coefficients $c_{v+f}$ (i.e. variable + fixed coefficients). The coefficient $c_{v+f}$ of the variable $z$ is omitted, because it has no bearing on product costs.

Final costing matrix:

| $c_{v+f}$ | | | 0 | | | |
|---|---|---|---|---|---|---|
| | | FX BND | 20 | | | |
| | | | $z$ | $r_o$ | $p_o$ | RHS |
| | $-f$ | | $-7.25$ | $-3.00$ | $-7.25$ | |
| $-2$ | $x_1$ | | $-.25$ | $-.333$ | $-.25$ | |
| $-3.50$ | $x_2$ | | $-.50$ | $-.667$ | $-.50$ | |
| | $y_1$ | | $-.75$ | | $-.75$ | |
| $-5$ | $y_2$ | | $-.25$ | | $-.25$ | |
| $-3.75$ | $y_3$ | | $-1$ | | $-1$ | |
| | $s$ | | $-.05$ | | $-.05$ | |

As we might have expected, costs prove to be £3.00 at the transfer point $R$ (Diagram 5), and £7.25 at point $P$. The techniques of linear algebra which I applied were not needed really to link the products made with corresponding sacrifices of producer goods. This applies also to the production system depicted in Exhibit 4[34].

The data in this exhibit are based on a problem that *Zionts* offers students as an exercise in linear programming. It concerns the manufacture of two brands of dog food, Albee and Bravo, which sell in 2 pound packages. The packaging facility operates at 15 seconds per package of Albee, and 10 seconds per package of Bravo. For the mixing and grinding of the ingredients there are separate facilities, which are not interchangeable. The percentages of water mixed into the dog foods are restricted to maxima. The quantities of meat scraps and meat by-products in Albee are restricted to minima, and the quantity of cereal in Bravo is restricted to a maximum.

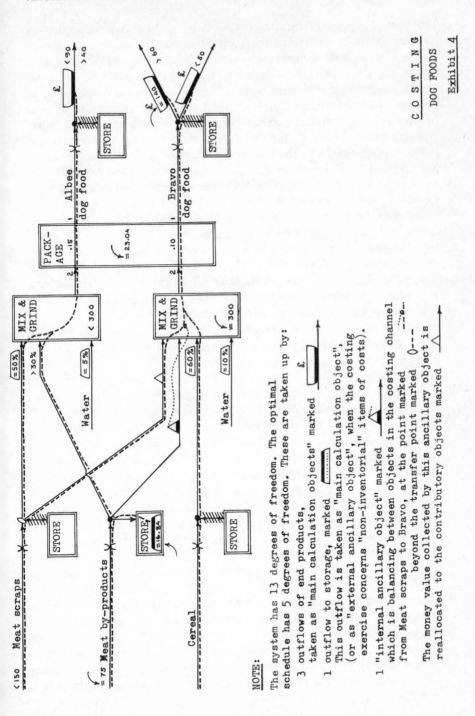

NOTE:

The system has 13 degrees of freedom. The optimal
schedule has 5 degrees of freedom. These are taken up by:

3  outflows of end products, taken as "main calculation objects" marked ▬▬▬

1  outflow to storage, marked ▬▬▬
   This outflow is taken as "main calculation object",
   (or as "external ancillary object", when the costing
   exercise concerns "non-inventorial" items of costs).

1  "internal ancillary object" marked ▬▬▬
   which is balancing between objects in the costing channel
   from Meat scraps to Bravo, at the point marked  0---
   beyond the transfer point marked  0---

   The money value collected by this ancillary object is
   reallocated to the contributory objects marked  △

The purchase price of meat by-products is expected to rise, so that an optimal schedule, calculated for successive months jointly, calls for an increase of the stock of meat by-products during the month of concern. It may be noted in passing that this flow into stock is a 'linking object' between the two successive schedules; it takes up 1 degree of freedom. 4 other degrees of freedom are taken up by the maximum availability of meat by-products, the limited capacities of the packaging facility and the mixing/grinding facility of Bravo, and the maximum outflow of Bravo along one of the marketing channels. The 8 remaining degrees of freedom of the system are taken up by 4 flows into stock with zero measure, and 4 quality constraints, as illustrated in Exhibit 4. Costing the scheduled measures of the two end products can be done without the aid of linear programming techniques, because it is self-evident which sacrifices of producer goods are to be associated with each of the 2 products. The point is, however, that the general procedure I have described, involving the choice of an internal ancillary object as shown in Exhibit 4, produces the correct product costs. One alternative ancillary object proves to be available, of much larger measure, namely the flow of meat scraps into Bravo, and this results quite naturally in the correct product costs also.

Such simple confirmation of correctness is not available for the costing of products from the oil refinery I described earlier on, because the link between product outflows and sacrifices of producer goods cannot be established in an alternative and simple manner. Carrying on from the Exhibit 3 and its associated trial costing matrix, it requires little imagination to conclude that the number of main products must be reduced from 5 to 3. This produces the costing structure shown in Exhibit 5. It is set up on the premises that Light distillate should be considered by-product, that the two Fuel oils should have equal status (as main product), and that Petrol should be the first main product to absorb the net value of internal ancillary objects. Starting from these premises the resultant product costs are uniquely defined, in spite of the alternative choices that are inherent to the procedure: The flow of Platformer bottoms into Petrol can be replaced as ancillary object by alternative flows into Petrol; the flow of Naphtha into Light distillate might be treated as an external instead of an internal ancillary object; and the costing channel of Petrol might be chosen along the flow of Light platformate instead of Heavy platformate. But none of these alternative ways of looking at things affects more than the relative flow values of some of the intermediate products used in the blending of Petrol; the product costs of the main products come out the same. The relation of these product costs to the directly traceable costs and proceeds in the production system can be expressed by a 'costing matrix', containing the relevant rows and columns of the end matrix reached in the costing exercise.

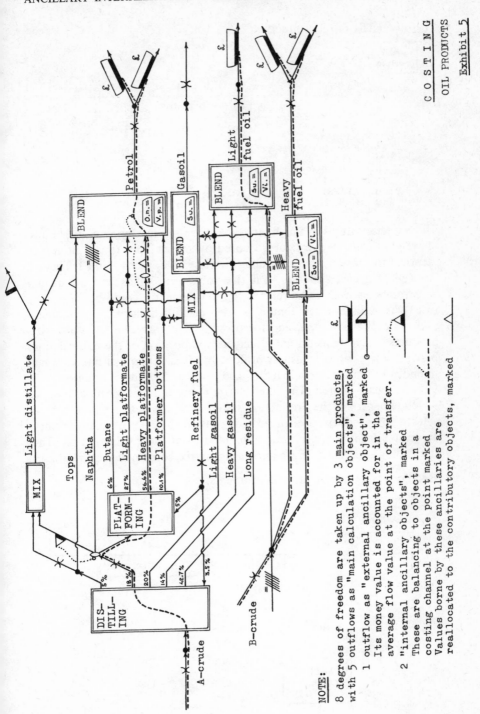

NOTE:

8 degrees of freedom are taken up by 3 main products, with 5 outflows as "main calculation objects", marked

1 outflow as "external ancillary object", marked ○. Its money value is accounted for in the average flow value at the point of transfer.

2 "internal ancillary objects", marked These are balancing to objects in a costing channel at the point marked Values borne by these ancillaries are reallocated to the contributory objects, marked

Costing matrix of oil products:

| Variable costs/proc | FX BND | .85 | 1.7444 | 1.2935 | Measures |
|---|---|---|---|---|---|
| | | PETROL | HY FUEL | LT FUEL | |
| | −f | −11.2919 | −1.5379 | −3.5307 | |
| −4.75 | A-CRUDE | −5.7647 | | | 4.90 |
| −1.15 | B-CRUDE | 2.2893 | −.9337 | −.5931 | .45 |
| −.20 | DISTILLER | −5.7647 | | | 4.90 |
| −.50 | PLTFORMER | −1.0190 | | | .8662 |
| 5.80 | LT DIST.1 | −.0706 | | | .06 |
| 5.50 | LT DIST.2 | −.1412 | | | .12 |
| 7.00 | GASOIL | −1.9907 | .0663 | .4070 | 1.05 |

The monetary items in this matrix are expressed in money units per unit of weight. The relative figures quoted by me as input to the model are identical to those in the scheduling exercise of Exhibits 1 and 2. They do not reflect a real situation, but the volumetric yields and the quality constraints, as well as the relative market demands, could be fairly realistic. I have disregarded charges for depreciation of assets, for remuneration on capital invested, and for prescribed margins on the sale of by-products. Such items do not affect the composition of the interrelations between the various measures of flow, but it is perhaps of interest that I intended to imply relatively high 'fixed' costs of B-crude, in addition to the variable costs quoted. The interrelations shown act as 'costing keys', by which expenses in the production system, and the net revenues from the sales of by-products, are traced indirectly to the sales of main products. Revenues from these sales are excluded from the costing matrix. They are quoted as input to the recompensing matrix, corresponding to Exhibit 6.

Recompensing matrix of oil investments:

| Variable costs/proc | FX BND | −.20 4.90 | −1.15 .45 | Measures |
|---|---|---|---|---|
| | | DISTILLER | B-CRUDE | |
| | −f | .9365 | 2.9660 | |
| −4.75 | A-CRUDE | −1 | | 4.90 |
| −.50 | PLTFORMER | −.1768 | | .8662 |
| 5.80 | LT DIST.1 | −.0122 | | .06 |
| 5.50 | LT DIST.2 | −.0245 | | .12 |
| 11.70 | PETROL.1 | −.0408 | | .20 |
| 10 | PETROL.2 | −.1327 | | .65 |
| 7 | GASOIL | −.2170 | .0300 | 1.05 |
| 5 | LT FUEL | −.2743 | .1125 | 1.2935 |
| 4.50 | HY FUEL.1 | −.0288 | −.1310 | .20 |
| 4.25 | HY FUEL.2 | −.2223 | −1.0115 | 1.5444 |

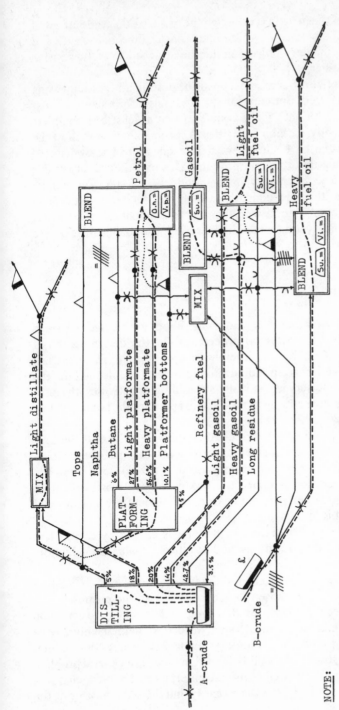

RECOMPENSING
INVESTMENTS IN OIL TRADE
Exhibit 6

NOTE:

This recompensing scheme is compatible with the production schedule and its 8 degrees of freedom. The scheme involves 2 **main investments**, all other investments being treated as "by-investments".

The main investment in distilling depends on A-crude as raw material, and on Petrol, Light fuel oil, Gasoil and Light distillate as principal products.
The other main investment depends on B-crude as raw material, and on the choice of Heavy fuel oil as principal product.

The composition of this matrix is based on the premises that the outflow of Heavy fuel oil should belong to the recompensing channel of B-crude, and that the 3 internal ancillary objects should be attached to recompensing channels of the distiller.

There is no essential difference between the costing and recompensing exercises that I described. Both are valuation exercises for a set of calculation objects. Both must satisfy the condition that at least one complete chain of independently variable activities is associable with each of the calculation objects chosen, beginning with the acquisition of a raw material and ending with the sale of an end product. To verify the validity of this chain, it is necessary to identify in the production system the linking objects, which act as the independently variable transferrers of value. Such linking objects, in combination with their correspondent transfer values, can serve to split the overall valuation exercise into a balancing exercise between subsystems.

## 3.8. RECAPITULATION

When the divisions of a company exchange goods or services between themselves, they ought to develop procedures for the determination of 'balanced transfer values' and 'indifferent linking objects'. Different sets of transfer values and corresponding linking objects are needed for the various purposes to be served, be it the scheduling of activities, the anticipatory or retrospective costing of products, or perhaps the recompensing of investments.

The transfer values are notional prices that apply equally to all divisions participating in the exchange at given geographical locations. At each location there is one division whose transaction has a zero net value. The volume of this transaction is called the linking object, which might be looked upon as the transferrer of value, or as the object for which internal supply and demand is in balance.

A proper balance at all locations of transfer is caused by correct forwarding of values at these locations, and results in a 'balanced valuation' of effective strains.

The types of strains to be valued, and the types of costs and proceeds to be taken into account, are chosen in accordance with the purpose being served. This purpose affects also the choice of 'ancillary calculation objects', or provisional recipients of value, needed to make the number of strains compatible with the production system and its degrees of freedom.

The valuation of strains in a well-balanced manner is a general problem of coordination in public as well as private enterprises. The balancing procedure described in this paper has the property that the act of measuring the values of strains is spread over the subsystems in which the strains occur. This type of approach is theoretically feasible, and will be considered sound by almost everyone with managerial responsibilities in a large organization.

## REFERENCES

[1] Arpan, J. S., *International Intracorporate Pricing. Non-American systems and views.* New York, 1971.
[2] Ashby, R. W., *Design for a Brain.* London, 1970.
[3] Balas, E., 'An infeasibility-pricing decomposition method for linear programs', *Operations Research* 14 (1966), 847–873.
[4] Baumol, W. J. and T. Fabian, 'Decomposition, pricing for decentralization and external economies', *Management Science* 11 (1964), 1–32.
[5] Baumol, W. J., 'Economic models and mathematics', *The Structure of Economic Science*, ed. S. R. Krupp. Englewood Cliffs, 1966.
[6] Bertalanffy, L. von, 'General system theory', *General Systems* 1 (1956).
[7] Boulding, K. E., 'General systems as a point of view', *Views on General Systems Theory*, ed. M. D. Mesarovic. London, 1964.
[8] Canning, R. G., *Electronic Data Processing.* New York, 1956.
[9] Conway, B., J. Gibbons, and D. E. Watts, *Business Experience and Electronic Computers.* New York, 1959.
[10] Dearden, J., 'Mirage of profit decentralization', *Harvard Business Review* 40 (1960), 140–154.
[11] DeMasi, R. J., *An Introduction to Business Systems Analysis.* Reading, 1969.
[12] Fawthrop, R. A., and G. Hayhurst, 'The cost of corporate planning constraints', *Proceedings I.F.A.C. Conference.* Paris, 1972.
[13] Hass, J. E., 'Transfer pricing in a decentralized firm', *Management Science* 14 (1968), B310–B331.
[14] Hayhurst, G., 'A corporate control system', *I.F.A.C. Workshop on Corporate Control Systems.* Enschede, 1974.
[15] Horngren, C. T., *Cost Accounting. A Managerial Emphasis.* Englewood Cliffs, 1972.
[16] Ijiri, Y., *The Foundations of Accounting Measurement. A Mathematical, Economic, and Behavioral Enquiry.* Englewood Cliffs, 1967.
[17] Klein Haneveld, A., *Notional Transfer Prices.* Unpublished Shell treatise, 1966.
[18] Klein Haneveld, A., *Decentralization and Decomposition.* Unpublished Shell treatise, 1969.
[19] Kreiken, J., 'Three dimensions of the management task', *Bedrijfskundig Bulletin T. H. Twente.* No. 3, 1971. Presidential address I.U.C. Congress, Brno, Czechoslowakia.
[20] Kreiken, J., *Management en Groei.* Enschede, 1973. Commemoration address T.H. Twente.
[21] Krens, F., *Interne Verrekenprijzen bij Gedivisionaliseerde Ondernemingen.* Leiden, 1975. Inaugural lecture Rotterdam.
[22] Lach, E. L., 'The total systems concept', *Systems and Procedures* 11, No. 4, Issue 44, 1960, pp. 6–7.
[23] McDonald, D. L., *Comparative Accounting Theory.* Reading, 1972.
[24] Mesarovic, M. D., D. Macko, and Y. Takahara, *Theory of Hierarchical, Multilevel Systems.* New York, 1970.
[25] Schroeff, H. J. v.d., *Kosten en Kostprijs.* Amsterdam, 1970. 2 vol.
[26] Shillinglaw, G., *Cost Accounting. Analysis and Control.* Homewood, 1972.
[27] Thompson, G. C., et al., 'Interdivisional transfer pricing', *Studies in Business Policy. National Industrial Conference Board.* No. 122, 1967.
[28] Unterguggenberger, S., *Cybernetica en Direct Costing.* Leiden, 1973.

[29] Verlage, H. C., *Transfer Pricing for Multinational Enterprises.* Rotterdam, 1975.

[30] Walker, W. E., 'A method for obtaining the optimal dual solution to a linear program using the Dantzig–Wolfe decomposition', *Operations Research* 17 (1969), 368–370.

[31] Wright, W. R., 'Direct costing – profit measurement', *N.A.A.–Bulletin.* Sept. 1959, Conference Proceedings.

[32] Wright, W. R., 'Direct costs are better for pricing', *N.A.A.–Bulletin.* April 1960.

[33] Young, B. J., 'Direct costing: accounting's contribution to improved management', *N.A.A.–Bulletin.* 1956/57, p. 362.

[34] Zionts, S., *Linear and Integer Programming.* Englewood Cliffs, 1974. (pp. 314–315).

# 4. Ratio network models and their application in budgeting

## C. VAN DER ENDEN

### 4.1. RATIO NETWORK MODELS

#### 4.1.1. Basic ideas

*a. Introduction*

Company models lay down the relationship between company results on the one hand and the factors which determine them on the other.

In the ratio network technique this relationship is laid down in a formalised scheme of relations between the various parameters which are here called *variables*.

The variables are represented by rectangles whereas relations existing between the variables are shown by arrows.

The direction of the arrow indicates the direction of the causal relation, which is in turn quantified by a *ratio* or proportional number.

Schematically:

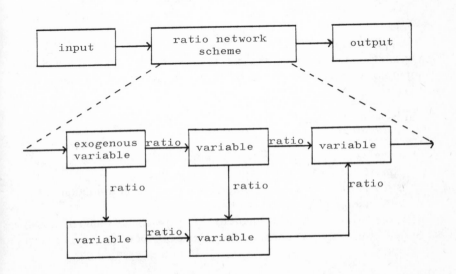

The relations are indicated step by step.

The use of the ratio network method for forecasting is based on the following empirical rules:

1. The ratio between connected variables is less liable to fluctuations than the variables themselves
2. The change in a ratio often shows a trend-like development, which can be summarised in a simple function
3. The constants of this function lend themselves to extrapolation in as far as they can be established by logical argument and they can, if need be, be adjusted on the basis of knowledge of the future.

### b. Structure

To build up a ratio network scheme the following questions must be asked:

– what are the relationships between the input data and the desired output data?
– how can these relationships be quantified?

The primary input data is an absolute parameter which usually indicates a level of activity, for instance sales or production volume for a period. These are exogenous variables: they are figures which indicate an expression for an activity, say sales, in the unit in which this activity is measured, for instance thousand pieces.

The relationships which exist between the parameters are the *ratios*.

The structure of the scheme is determined by stating step by step the relationships between the exogenous and the other – endogenous – variables.

A simple *example*.

Question: How many of the persons depending on the production volume do we need on an average in a year, assuming that stocks are constant?

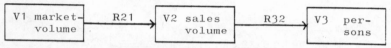

V1 is the exogenous variable which indicates the total market volume expected in a given year, expressed in product units

R21 is the market share of the enterprise expressed in a fraction of the total market, going from 0 to 1

R32 is the labour coefficient, that is to say the personnel required in man years – directly dependent on the volume of production – per product unit.

The exogenous variable and the ratios R21 and R32 are the input data.
    The volume of sales and the number of persons, the variables, are the output data.
    An example in *figures* is:

    V1  = 12,000 pieces
    R21 = 0.15 (15%)
    R32 = 0.5

From the ratio network we then obtain:

    V2 = 12,000 × 0.15 = 1,800 pieces
    V3 = 1,800 × 0.5 = 900 persons.

*c. Notation*

The notation is obtained by two rules:

1. Multiplication of the variable at the origin of the arrow by the corresponding ratio gives the value of the arrow and with it the value of the variable determined by the arrow.
2. If a variable is determined by a number of other variables, then it is indicated by a number of arrows. The value of that variable is then equal to the sum of the values of the arrows concerned.

*Example*:

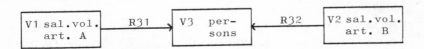

Example in *figures*:

    V1  = 180 pieces
    V2  = 120 pieces
    R31 = 5
    R32 = 6

N.B. V1 and V2 are calculated in another part of the scheme.

From the network it follows that:

    V3 = 180 × 5 + 120 × 6 = 900 + 720 = 1,620 persons.

### 4.1.2. Input data

#### a. Survey

The input data consist of the *ratio values* and exogenous variables for the future period or – if the calculation has to cover a number of periods – for the future periods. These are discussed in paragraphs c. and d. Sometimes the *initial values* of *variables* which occur in the scheme have to be taken into account: they, too, then become input data.

In mechanical computation the length of the period and the number of periods to be calculated must be included in the input data.

#### b. Endogenous variables

The period has the following function:

– *flow* variables and the ratios referring to them are measured over the duration of these periods, for instance sales
– *state* variables or levels and the ratios connecting them are measured at the end of the period, for instance stocks.

The value the variable can assume can be:

1. *random*, for instance the weight of raw materials stock
2. a *multiple* of a *unit*, for instance the number of products in stock
3. a *multiple* of a *given number*, such as the capacity of a factory with machines linked in parallel (for instance a multiple of 4) or the extension of floor space by a minimum step size (for instance a multiple of 500 m²).
   In this case the desired 'rounding-off' must be entered as a ratio
4. *binary* ratio, that is to say 0 or 1.
   These are the so-called logical variables, in which 0 means 'no, does not satisfy the formulated equation' and 1 means 'yes, does satisfy'. These variables ensure that, depending upon the situation, the correct computation rules of the scheme are applied.

#### c. Exogenous variables

These are absolute amounts.
Examples:

– market volume
– sales volume
– fixed personnel (man years per period).

These are variables which cannot be calculated from the relationships laid down in the scheme. As they are input data they are described as exogenous variables.

### d. Actual ratios

These are proportional numbers which can be classified according to their dimension.

### 4.1.3. Dimensions

Notation: Q = quantity (volume)
T = time
M = money

### a. Dimension Q/Q

The ratio between two quantities at a given time. In the ratio network schemes only a related form of this occurs: see sub *b*.

### b. Dimension $\dfrac{Q1/T}{Q2/T} = \dfrac{Q1}{Q2}$

The ratio between two flows in a given period of time, both expressed in quantity.

As a flow has dimension Q/T (quantity per time), the dimension of the

ratio between two flows is $\dfrac{Q1}{Q2}$.

Examples of this frequently occurring type of ratio:
– energy consumption per machine hour
– fuel consumption per kilometre travelled
– raw material consumption per product manufactured
– days of sickness as a fraction of the theoretical number of working days.

The fact is often neglected that these ratios are ratios between flows measured over a given period. They are then used as quantity ratios (see *a*.)

### c. Dimension $\dfrac{Q}{Q/T}$

The ratio between a level and a flow must be handled carefully. The difficulty is the relationship between the point in time of the level and the period over which the flow is measured.

Examples:

– stock ratio: ratio per unit of sale in the period ahead
– ratio of the sales level to actual sales in which the time level is the middle of the selling period.

*d. Dimension* M/Q

A well known ratio is that between an amount of money and a quantity: it is a price.

*e. Dimension* $\dfrac{M/T}{Q/T}$

When a price has a time element we have a ratio between an amount of money over a period and a service covering a period.
Examples:

– wages per year / man years per year
– rents per year / use covering the period of a year.

*f. Dimension* M/M = 1

This is a ratio between two financial levels, for instance the ratio between equity and total capital employed.

*g. Dimension* $\dfrac{M/T}{M/T} = 1$

The ratio between two financial flows, for instance that between paid interest and the use of capital, being the rate of interest.

*h. Dimension* $\dfrac{M}{M/T}$

For instance the debtor ratio is one between a financial level and the financial flow over a period. Here the claim at a time (for instance end of the year) is expressed in sales over a preceding period (1 year).

*i. Units*

Care should be taken to ensure consistent use of a unit once it has been selected. Quantities can be expressed in number, area, content, weight, time, etc.

   For instance, once we have decided on 'thousand pieces' as the unit of quantity for the product and on 'one thousand guilders' as the monetary unit, we must express the price of the product in thousands guilders per thousand pieces, which is of course equal to guilders each.

*4.1.4. Relationships*

*a. Relationships between variables*

1. Within the period

These are usually taken to be linear according to the well-known function:

$$y = a \times x + b$$

Here $y$ and $x$ are variables, $a$ is a coefficient and $b$ an exogenous variable.
In the ratio network scheme:

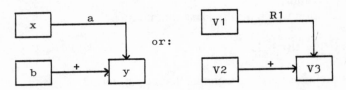

Non-linear functions can also be used, provided it is possible to make their occurrence logically acceptable; otherwise it is pointless.

## 2. Between the periods

We often find this dynamic relationship involving:
– the influence of the past on the present:
the size of the stock of the previous period has an influence on present day production volume
– the influence of the future on the present:
the volume of sales of the period ahead determines the required level of stock of the present period.

In the first case the respective variables of the period preceding the period of time to be calculated must be included in the input data.

In the second case we must include the value of the ratio or exogenous variable of the period following the period to be calculated as an input data.

## b. *Relationships between the ratios*

## 1. Within the period

In the ideal case the ratio values of a given period should be completely independent of one another. In practice this is impossible; we know very well that there is a dependence, but nevertheless we are unable to quantify it.

Let us take as an example market share and selling price as input data.

At a given total market, it is – ceteris paribus – usually true that a higher selling price reduces the market share.

If the relationship were to be described in terms of a mathematical formula – as is the case in physical laws – then it should be possible to replace the ratio of the market share by a function of the ratio of the selling price or vice versa. As the relationship cannot, however, be given as a formula, we have to use two ratios and in every individual case ask how the values will relate to one another.

2. Between the periods

As has been remarked in *a.*, the trend of a ratio can often be described in a simple function.

The function which occurs most commonly is

$$R(t) = R(t - 1) \times (1 + d)$$

in which *d* indicates the fractional change per period.

Here *d* can assume the following values:

- $d = 0$               : the ratio is constant
- $d$ = between $-1$ and $0$ : the ratio drops according to a geometric series
- $d$ = positive       : the ratio rises according to a geometric series.

The future value of the factor *d* must be estimated from:

- the trend in the past, which can be calculated by division of the variables
- the change in the situation in the future.

c. *Comparison with other mathematical models*

1. No optimization, as is the case in mathematical programming, but simulation.
2. Characteristics are not a result, as is the case in the Du Pont model[1], but aids in forecasting.
3. No chronological scheme, as in network planning, but a functional scheme to be used again in every period and one with which the variables are computed time-dependently and dynamically.
4. No restriction to linear relationships, as in linear programming; indeed the use of other functional relationships is possible.


4.1.5. *Application*

a. *Steps to be taken in practice*

In practice it is necessary first to find out whether there is already a standard model for the problem to be solved. In many cases it is possible, by adjusting the input data, to save the time necessary for a specific model and one can start with step 2.

1. Construction of a system of equations using the notation described above
2. Determining the value of the variables in the preceding period(s)
3. Determining the value of the ratios in the preceding period from the variables
4. Determining the future change to be expected in the ratio values
5. Computing the value of the variables per period.

Should a computer be used, the comparison described under 1. above must be programmed, for instance in FORTRAN.

Thus:

gives the statement:

$$V(2, t) = V(1, t) * R(1, t)$$

In that case the input values obtained are punched as step 5 or keyed at the terminal.

### b. *Instructions for model building*

#### 1. Detailing

There are two dangers here. First of all, with excessive simplification an inadequate picture of the problem is obtained which leads to faulty decisions. Secondly, if the construction is too complicated, the model becomes unmanageable because too many input data are required and clarity is lost.

Use only causal relationships and no indirect relationships. The use of other than linear relationships must be partly based on knowledge of the real situation and not purely on statistical analysis.

Exaggerated insistence on accuracy can be avoided if one ensures:

– the necessary tolerance in the input data
– the permissible tolerance in the output data: it will not lead to wrong decisions if for example the outcome of a present value calculation is + 120 or + 180, as long as it is positive.

#### 2. Definitions

The ratio, as regards content, must connect up with the variables. From this it follows that variables have to be well defined.

A statement such as 'there is a three months' stock' can mean a number of things:

1. three preceding months' sales
2. three future months' sales (better)
3. three months based on the moving annual total, that is one and a half months' sales immediately preceding and one and a half months' future sales
4. inclusive or exclusive of seasonal stock.

### 3. Documentation

Without good documentation all the trouble expended on a model is completely wasted. Such documentation must at least include:

- definition of ratios
- definition of variables
- ratio network scheme
- form for input data
- worked out example with input and output data
- statement of eventual existing computer programs and of addresses where these are to be obtained with the documentation
- statement of number and date of release of the programs.

### c. *Instructions for use*

Both the ratios and the output data must be oriented towards the use made of the model at a later time. The whole must appeal to the user and must lend itself to practical discussion. Only in that way can decision-taking be improved.

As many as possible of the forecast parameters must subsequently be measured against the real value. In this way the model maker and the providers of input data can check whether they can achieve even better performance in model construction and value estimation.

The following compromise will have to be made between the desirable and the possible:

- on the one hand an adaptation of the data established by the accounting department to the variables in the model;
- on the other hand an adaptation of the variables in the model to the data provided by the accounting department.

### d. *Use of the computer*

Use of the computer is made possible by writing the network in a computer language, as stated in *a*.

The advantages are the following:

1. simulation of a large number of alternative plans is possible
2. simulation of several external possibilities
3. sensitivity analyses
4. rapid and faultless computation
5. low costs.

For practical use of ratio network models a (small) computer is preferable to an office calculator.

The conversion of the network to a computer program is not difficult.

## e. Fields of application

Ratio networks can, in addition to simulation, be used in many other ways for decision-taking in the enterprise:

1. Long-term period plans
2. Long-term project plans
3. Budgeting for one or more years
4. Sensitivity analysis
5. Adjustment of partial plans to total plans
6. Convenient aid in illustrating complicated relationships
7. Systematizing model building
8. Basis for computer programs.

Once models have been made they are easily adapted to changed needs or circumstances.

## f. Restrictions

1. The 'ceteris paribus' assumption on input of new values of a ratio leads to a saving in input data. However, one must bear in mind that this assumption must also be correct in concrete cases. If there is a clear-cut relationship between ratios this must be taken into account as far as possible.
2. The presentation of the development of the ratios by a geometric series also ensures a saving of input data. These series, however, exclude the forecasting of a bending point in the development. In long-term forecasts in particular one must find out whether there are indications for such a bending point.
3. Simulation makes it possible to obtain simple models, but involves the need to seek the correct alternative. Here it will often only be possible to approximate to the actual optimum. The question is, however, whether this is not also the case with the programs for optimum calculations, as in linear programming.

## g. Conclusion

The ratio network approach with its simple goal-directed models and its short time for constructing has proved its value in practical use within the Philips Group. Models are designed and in use for decision calculation, for prognosis of product divisions and countries and for factory budgeting as well.

We have learnt that models as a tool of limited scope dedicated to a specific function are of real value for management. They offer a way of escaping from the comprehensive corporate model ('from the bottom up' or 'from the top down') before it becomes a Frankenstein monster.[2]

## 4.2. BUDGETING WITH THE HELP OF THE RATIO NETWORK METHOD

### 4.2.1. Introduction

The aspects of the company and, hence, of the inherent decision-making process are manifold. It will suffice for us to distinguish between four of them:

– activities
– functions
– geographical distribution
– time.

These aspects should be given consideration before a start is made on constructing a useful calculation model. Dependent on the organization of the company or part thereof, and determined by the object we pursue, we shall arrive at certain conclusions with respect to the demarcation and detailing of each aspect.

## a. Activities

The activities undertaken by the company for the market consist in the selling of products and services. In large companies, the organization is often based on a division of the activities according to products, the various business units bearing such names as product division, industry group, project group, etc. The activities may also be divided according to clientèle:

– industry
– wholesale business
– retail business.

In comparatively smaller companies the product aspect is likewise indispensable in judging the product range. The desirability of launching new products and terminating the production of current products can only be judged from this angle.

### b. Functions

As regards the division into functions we have in mind particularly the 'internal business column', i.e. the successive abilities required to offer products (and services) to the selling market. The main functions are:

1. *Research:*

    General research into further potentialities of the company, not only in the technical but also in the commercial field.

    A distinction as made with respect to the activities mentioned against *a*. applies to research only in part.

2. *Development:*

    Development for application of new products, means and methods.

3. *Production:*

    The manufacture of products; here a further organizational distinction can be made, both according to technology and product.

4. *Distribution:*

    Bringing the products to the consumers, with all the aspects involved.

### c. Geographical distribution

When one of the functions mentioned under *b.* is performed in different territories, distinction will be made into economic blocks (e.g. E.E.C.), countries, regions or locations.

In particular for activities in different *countries* there will be local organizational units. In view of the fact that the activity aspect *a.*is never non-existent, there arises a matrix organization. Each local organization is then organized according to the various activities or product groups.

The management of such a product group has contacts with all similar product groups, while central management maintains contact with all countries.

### d. Time

All activities are performed in the time sphere and all decisions make their effect felt during a certain period of time. Any surveyable period is called the planning horizon: the decision-maker should position himself at such a 'high' observation post that the horizon will be sufficiently far distant for him, enabling him to overlook the whole relevant period of time.

We shall use the time aspect for the classification of management activities.

### 4.2.2. Management activities

The demarcation lines between the various types of planning are not clear-cut because there is an interplay between plans for the long term and for the short. The resulting adaptation of plans, however, should not take place too frequently in order not to upset the course of business, but the plans must not be continued without modification until they swerve all too much from reality.

The object of planning and budgeting is to preserve the continuity of the company by:

- reporting dangers in good time
- early detection of new openings
- early choice from alternatives (sometimes a provisional choice)
- delegation to a lower level of management with the appertaining authorization to take decisions, including expenditure.

*a. The strategic plan* determines the company's field of activity for the very long term, e.g. 20 years. In most cases, it is a limitation in terms of

- activities which will be offered in the market
- functions which the company will perform within these activities, e.g. manufacturing a product internally or not, acting as a retailer or not
- fields to be operated in, e.g. export, production abroad, or otherwise.

*b. The project plans* relate to those activities which fit into the framework of the strategic plan. Tracing these activities and formulating a project as a combination thereof, presupposes also:

1. Research into the technical possibilities, which may be seen as finalization of the technical research referred to under *a*.
2. Research into the commercial possibilities as a result of the commercial research referred to under *a*.

The evaluation comprises the weighing of alternative projects. It aims at predicting the consequences of the possible performance of the project. In most cases, there will be alternative ways of carrying out the project, all of which must be reviewed.

In addition it will be necessary to judge the coexistence within the company. We refer to the joint influence which the projects exert on the company in the form of:

- tie-up of means of production
- unavailability of specific groups of personnel for other jobs, e.g. for product development
- tie-up of capital
- results expected per period; if too many projects are simultaneously in the starting-up stage they may result in a too unsatisfactory profitability in a given period, even if they are profitable individually.

This appraisal for coexistence happens by means of period plans, for which the project plans provide the details.

*c. The period plans* comprise all activities of the company or part thereof during a medium term, e.g. 4 years. The length of this period depends primarily on the preparational period for the acquisition of the production factors.

The chemical industry, which is very capital intensive, requires a longer horizon than an assembly works which is in a position to acquire sufficient universally usable floor space and personnel.

The ideal way in which a period plan can be prepared is a consolidation of the project plans. Period plans however, at least in part, will be based in practice on *preliminary* decisions, during which it is nevertheless possible to prepare a consistently overall plan by way of a systematic approach.

The period plan is the framework for further operational decisions.

*d. Operational plans*

Based on project plans, and within the framework of period plans, numerous operational decisions must be taken on the procedure to be adopted.

For the medium and short term (1 to 4 years) it should be ascertained whether or not the manufacturing process will be carried out with or without particular automatic equipment, in shifts or otherwise, in large or small batches, etc.

We have now reached the border line between innovation and routine.

The alternatives are evaluated as described against *b.* for projects. Now, however, the economic criterion will not always be formulated in terms of maximum present value of net receipts. Given particular receipts, a minimum present value of the *expenses* will often be concerned.

The operational plans, after having been decided on and approved, will be made the basis of the budgets.

### e. Annual budgets

Detailed plans which cover only one period are often referred to as budgets. The technique of budgeting will be discussed in section 4.2.3.

Budgets have a similar function as the period plan but they are

- more detailed
- task-setting
- giving authority (to make payments)
- a means for making a subsequent check on the course of business.

The annual budgets are based on operational plans, which, however, can in turn be revised by feedback effects before the annual budget is established definitely.

The annual budgets as a means of delegation are – more obviously than the period plans – a framework for the further performance decisions and a means of communication, in particular for the lower level of management.

### f. Implementation and reporting

From the very short to the short term – from a few hours to one year – it is necessary to take decisions which are often designated as 'routine'.

However, this refers rather to their multiplicity than to their uniformity. In particular decisions for the very short term often have no financial criterion. Sometimes there is no alternative and the decision is in fact a reaction to an external or internal event. Sometimes there are no financial consequences because the effect of the decision for the very short term on the expenditure is negligible.

To the extent that there are financial consequences, discounting can in general be dispensed with. Assuming a minimum required rate of return of 10% after tax for example, the adjustment resulting from discounting will often be much smaller than the error arising from estimation.

Examples of decisions at the performance level are:

1. increase or reduce the selling price of the product temporarily
2. overtime
3. shorter hours
4. make, or buy, components for the time being.

Such decisions might be called micro-decisions. They affect the actual results to be compared with the budget.

In that way the budget is a yardstick. Deviations – both upwards and downwards – should be explained by those who are responsible for them.

Hence, each detail budget has one budget holder: un budget c'est un monsieur (a budget is a person). It is self-evident that, in preparing the annual budget, account must be taken of this control function of the budget.

Financial reporting may be the reason to change the measures agreed upon. This may be due to internal or external circumstances.

One of the major problems in reporting in big concerns is how to reach the objective: motivating the personnel towards taking those actions which are in the interest of the entire company.

A shift in the organization structure from a functional (purchase, development, production, selling) structure to a product-oriented one may solve the problem in part. The set-up of product-oriented teams (article teams) is therefore gaining ground. These teams judge the effectiveness of an overall market-oriented activity in terms of the company objective.

This effectiveness is measured by evaluating the integral project and is expressed in the excess of net capital worth over the required minimum rate of return (project evaluation).

The appraisal of the performance of the various functions, e.g. the measurement of the degree of efficiency of the operations, is a different matter. Any efficient production of articles which falls short of required minimum profitability is ineffective.

On the other hand, an activity may be effective despite an inefficient production and commercial organization. This happens, among other things, in monopolistic situations.


### 4.2.3. The budget: basic ideas

#### a. Justification

Every year a lot of work is done in numerous companies – partly in overtime – in order to prepare the annual budget for each department.

It may be worth asking oneself whether the time devoted by managers and accountants could be spent to better advantage by a systematic approach and the use of a computer.

The present situation of a lot of budgets is that of a type of accounting system with numerous transfers and allocations. Thus the interest of many departmental heads is often confined to 'taking care to keep out of the red figures in the later post-calculation'.

When asking ourselves what is the ultimate justification of budgeting, the answer we find, just like in the case of any other project in the company is: the increase of the net cash flow. As a budget is not based on receipts and payments and (in most cases) not prepared per project, it is not an *immediate* instrument for decisions concerning projects. An annual reconsideration of the course of business and annual discussions with the officials concerned are essential to keep the company on the right course. In this way, the course is indicated in which the company should trend, tasks are set and accepted, weaknesses are discovered and remedied, authorization is given and a basis is laid for reporting.

### b. Specific objectives

A practical approach to the present alternatives results in the following specification:

1. The discussions in the company on the budget data should in the first place concern *quantitative* relations in their functional aspects. Financial data only come up for discussion when making a choice from alternatives, in the form of future cash flows.

   *Example*
   Maintenance of machines is not discussed in terms of guilders per year or per operating hour. The quantities concerned here are hours and materials consumed (as a fraction of the machine). The functional relationships depend on the organization of the maintenance work and the nature of the equipment. The maintenance may depend on the number of operating hours, of available hours, or of both. All this appeals much more to a departmental head than the usual $x$ thousand guilders which is negotiated as annual costs.

2. Calculating the budget with the aid of fast calculating machines in the case of changes in:

   – production package
   – structure of the manufacturing process
   – prices.

   In this way, one is confronted in time with the consequences for capacity utilization, task setting and cost prices.

3. Opportunity for inter-firm comparison with similar manufacturing processes and of reporting which is directed at the facts–i.e. at the quantities. We note at once, however, that the budget is not in general suitable for the measurement of individual performance. The reporting (post-calculation) indicates variances from budget, but unfavourable variances may be over-compensated by favourable variances in other departments or even in other sectors of the company. It is also possible that favourable variances are over-compensated by unfavourable ones elsewhere.

### c. Approach

Even more than before, the budget will have to be based on the interrelations within the company. The tasks of the various departments should be laid down, together with the activities or situations which determine the volume of these tasks.

For some companies, this may mean a kind of examination of the organization. In order to ensure clarity and simplicity, it is advisable to take into account some rules.

Divide all activities in the 3 usual categories:

1. Production departments, which supply performances or services directly to the products.
   N.B. Where products are referred to, this term is interchangeable with: services to be supplied to the market.

2. Auxiliary departments, supplying services to the production departments and – in particular cases – to the products. They do *not* supply any services among themselves.
   In many companies, services supplied between auxiliary departments are charged mutually. This procedure is at variance with the fact that auxiliary departments may derive their right to exist from services for production departments and not from mutual servicing.
   Moreover, these entries provide extra work and veil the normal course of business.

   *Examples*

   planning, administration, management, stores.

3. Auxiliary cost centres, which supply services to one another, to auxiliary departments and production departments. These cost centres often have an administrative character and should be budgeted in a particular order of succession on account of the mutual deliveries.
   For instance:
   1. personnel costs
   2. housing costs: on the basis of personnel costs
   3. costs of power: on the basis of personnel costs and housing costs.

### 4.2.4. The budget: flow-chart

The figure on the next page illustrates that the processing of the data in the case of *quantitative* budgeting may be represented by 8 stages; the other 7 stages concern the processing of financial data.

Although the principles applying to all sectors of the company are alike, we shall refer to a production unit with the appertaining auxiliary departments and auxiliary cost centres.

The relations are always as follows:
a. A department renders *services*, either to products, or to other departments, e.g. the turning of a steel spindle.
b. These services require *activities*, e.g.
  1 hour's use of a turning lathe, and
  2 man-hours for turning and finishing.
c. These activities entail the use of *capacity*.
d. Both the activities and the capacities require:
  1. services by third parties
  2. services by auxiliary departments (see *a.*)
  3. services by auxiliary cost centres (see *a.*).
The arrows in the chart indicate the relations, which can be divided into:
1. activities per service, per product   }[3]
2. capacities per type, per activity      }
3. services per type, per activity and
   services per type, per capacity
4. prices of third parties.
These relations are represented in matrices or sets of figures.

*Example*
If 2 products are processed which require 1 and 3 machine-hours and 2 and 5 man-hours, respectively, the matrix for the activities will be:

|               | *Prod. 1* | *Prod. 2* |
|---------------|-----------|-----------|
| Machine-hours | 1         | 3         |
| Man-hours     | 2         | 5         |

Step 1. *Products*
A list of products to be manufactured, or production plan: quantities per product.

Step 2. *Direct materials*
With the aid of a matrix R21 'quantities per product' the direct materials per product and per type of materials are calculated.
  Direct materials denote all materials and services from third parties which can be allocated directly to the product. It is not customary to include these in the departmental expenses, but it is advisable to mention them in the budget.

Step 3. *Activities (tie-up of capacity) and capacities of production departments*
With the help of the matrix R31 'activities per product' the primary production activities are calculated for each type of activity. We shall refer to a department or sub-department yielding a particular type of performance as a *group*.

## FLOWCHART QUANTITIES BUDGET

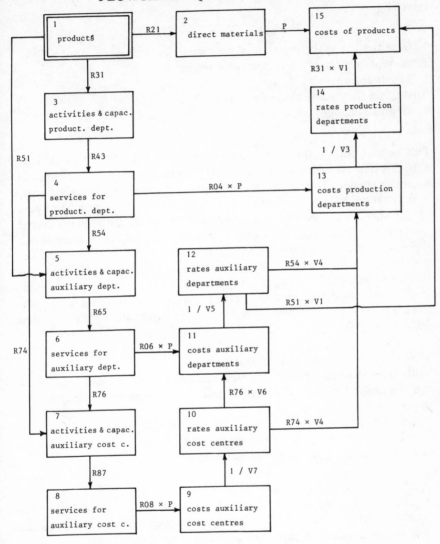

P = external prices

Such a group might, for instance, perform assembly work of a particular level or turning on a particular type of turning lathe. The required capacities are calculated from the activities by means of another matrix: number of employees, machines, space.

The capacity entails a problem: it is not always possible to adjust the actually available production factors to the required production factors within the available time.

The volume of the available means of production is indeed partly determined by:

1. the situation at the moment of preparing the budget
2. current agreements, e.g. contracts already concluded
3. the fact that in the case of increase of capacity, stepwise changes will occur.

This applies both in the case of an excess and in the event of a shortage.

In this step a confrontation takes place between the required (calculated) means of production and the expected average position in the budget year.

When there is a shortage, the production plan must be revised, or a part of the work should be sub-contracted to third parties, with the result that the activities (step 3) decrease and the need for capacity diminishes. When there is an excess, the capacity is underloaded. In most cases, this concerns buildings, machines and personnel, but in special cases supply contracts for raw materials, for example, may worsen the situation.

The rates are determined in a later stage on the basis of requirements; the expected position serves for estimating the total costs and the expected losses arising from underload.

## Step 4. *Services for production departments*

With the aid of the matrix R43 'services per group" we can derive how much is needed in terms of activities and capacities and what this requires in terms of:
− materials and services from third parties via R04
− services by auxiliary departments via R54
− services by auxiliary cost centres via R74.

## Step 5. *Activities and capacities of auxiliary departments*

With the help of matrices R51 and R54 for activities of auxiliary departments per service to the production department we determine the required activities and, next, the capacities in the auxiliary departments.

For, these make it possible to use the (primary) production factors in the production departments, even if the relation is not always a direct one.

It will be necessary in one's own company to search for the relations by asking oneself what is the task of the various auxiliary departments.

In many cases departments must be divided into groups with a particular type of performance (see step 3). To this end, (temporary) self-recording of hours devoted to particular jobs and interviews may be useful. A few well-known relations are:

- number of employees in production department ──→activities for wage accounting and for canteen facilities
- quantity of materials consumed ──→ (by way of stock and lot size) activities for purchase, storage and internal transport
- number of sq.m. or cub.m. housing ──→activities for maintenance.

Sometimes it will be necessary to establish a rather arbitrary relation between auxiliary groups and production activities, but might the lack of relation not be caused by an indistinct organization or by activities which are continued because they hold out a vague promise for the future?

For particular departments, notably in the development sector, there is a *distinct* relation with future production. These departments are budgeted separately on the basis of expected activities. Their costs are not charged to the current production, but are carried through a balance-sheet account.

As already observed, the auxiliary departments in the production sector derive their right to exist exclusively from the production departments and can only justify their costs on the grounds of support to the production. In this reasoning, there is no room for the so-called horizontal charges among auxiliary departments. We make an exception for some specialized functions, such as providing accommodation, which render services to both auxiliary and to production departments.

These are the auxiliary cost centres (step 7). The model indicates the possibility that particular activities of the auxiliary departments can be related directly with products (arrows 12–15).

Step 6. *Services for auxiliary departments*
The matrix R65 transforms the activities and capacities into services, just as described in step 4 for the production departments.

The services come from
- third parties via R06
- auxiliary cost centres via R76.

Step 7. *Activities and capacities of auxiliary cost centres*
These are derived from the required services to:
1. production departments via R74
2. auxiliary departments via R76.

Step 8. *Services for auxiliary cost centres*
The activities are now transformed with matrix R87 into services required by auxiliary cost centres.

This completes the quantitative part of the budget. Prices from third parties – i.e. from outside the circle budgeted for – have not been used so far.

Step 9. *Costs of auxiliary cost centres*
In calculating the costs of auxiliary departments, just like those of other
departments, distinction should be made between:

a. costs of activities which normally can be adapted in the budget to the
   volume of activities
b. costs of capacities for which in principle a temporary difference is
   permissible.

The costs are established by multiplying the services received according to
R08 by the purchase prices.

Step 10. *Rates of auxiliary cost centres*
The costs of services required for *activities* are divided by the expected
activities for the purpose of determining the rate of a group.
    The costs of *capacities* on the other hand are divided by the 'normal'
activities. These have been set at a certain percentage (e.g. 80%) of the
activity to be performed with the available capacity[4].

*Example*
One machine can normally supply 1,600 hours activity in each year. In
view of a normative underload of 20%, the normal capacity will be 0.8 ×
1,600 hours = 1,280 hours.
    The costs of the machine are divided by this last-mentioned number of
hours.
    In so far as the machine employment involves costs which may vary with
a more direct activity, these must be allocated directly to this activity or
product.
    If for instance 1 kwh of electricity *per product* is consumed, this unit of
energy must be regarded as direct production factor, i.e. as direct materials
(step 2).
    Every time causal relationships must be established, so that the budget
can serve upon completion – i.e. within certain limits – as a company
(calculation) model.
    Thus the rate per activity consists of:

1. direct expenses for activities, divided by the expected activity, *plus*:
2. expenses for capacities, divided by the normal activity.

Step 11. *Costs of auxiliary departments*
These are made up of:
a. services by third parties times price
b. services by auxiliary cost centres times rate, as per step 10.

Step 12. *Rates of auxiliary departments*
The same calculation as referred to against 10.

Step 13. *Costs of production departments*
There are 3 types of services:

*a.* services by third parties times price
*b.* services by auxiliary departments times rate as per step 12
*c.* services by auxiliary cost centres times rate as per step 10.

Step 14. *Rates of production departments*
The same calculation as referred to against 10.

Step 15. *Costs of products*
The price of a product is built up of 3 elements:

1. direct materials times price
2. activities by production departments per product times rate as per step 14
3. services by auxiliary departments per product times rate as per step 12.

SUMMARY

The budget is prepared according to the ratio network method on the basis of:

*a.* quantity of products
*b.* technical ratios for transformation of activities into capacities and services
*c.* prices per unit of materials and services by third parties
*d.* available production factors.

The coefficients mentioned under *b.* have been used twice:

1. for the determination of the activities of the departments which supply the services
2. for the calculation of the costs of the departments which make use of these services, i.e. by multiplication with the rates.

NOTES

1. Executive Committee Control Charts, published by Du Pont de Nemours, 1959.
2. See 'What kind of corporate modeling functions best?', by Robert H. Hayes and Richard L. Nolan, *HBR* May-June 1974, page 102.
3. Compressed in flowchart to save space.
4. This attainable activity is tantamount to the well-known concept 'available, rational and harmonious capacity'.

# 5. The development of a budgeting model*

H. A. SMITS and P. A. VERHEYEN

## 5.1. INTRODUCTION

Dutch States Mines (DSM) have devised a mathematical model for company-wide budgeting and made it operational as part of their integrated system of management information, financial accounting and business control.

In the following description, emphasis will be on the model's historical development in its several phases in order to show the logic underlying their sequence. A brief look is also given to the operational model used at present. The model's success as a regular operating tool can be explained from the fact that nowhere at the various stages of its introduction was the contact with the users lost, constant regard being paid to what they could accomplish in their own practical situation.

In describing the two practical applications of the model in a historical context, reference to the underlying principles will be made in broad terms. The appendix gives a generalized version in mathematical form.

## 5.2. THE PRELIMINARY PHASE

The budgeting system DSM operated in the early sixties pivoted on cost allocation. Primary costs and revenues were assessed per cost centre and manually charged to others using the principle of cause and effect.

The system had some serious disadvantages:

– Budgeting for hundreds of cost centres spread over a number of plants and general services will require a large accounting force if it is basically a pencil-and-paper job.
– Planners are highly dependent on each other, the output of one cost centre being the input of another. Frequent adjustment of internal transfers and prices will, therefore, be necessary in an attempt to make intermediate-product and energy balances tally.

* The authors thank P. Adams, Dr. J. Th. C. van Lieshout and J. H. J. Roemen for their critical remarks.

– If prices of inputs change, proper adaptation of the entire budget is hardly feasible because of the multiple relationships between cost centres and the sheer magnitude of the resulting figure-handling.

The above drawbacks can be largely overcome, if the computer can take the data-processing off the accountant's hands, a development for which conditions were favourable with DSM in 1965:

– The idea of massive data processing was not new to the company, 35 years of experience having accrued to it from punched-card systems for various accounting functions.
– A trust-relationship had been established between managers, engineers, and accountants in the field of budgetary control.
– The first sizeable computer (Univac III) had just been installed.

## 5.3. THE CONCEPTUAL SIDE

With DSM the stimulus for a more fundamental approach to the budgeting problem came from an article written by Hershey and Schwartz (1957)[1] on cost roll-up as adopted by Du Pont. On the basis of an existing elaborate cost pattern, the latter firm had prepared special software to compute the accumulated (rolled-up) primary-cost structure of end products. Thus, this technique permitted of a rapid calculation of the effects on intermediate and end product prices of any change in input prices or production volume. The article showed how accumulated primary cost can be computed, once the cost pattern has been analyzed to the required level of detail.

As distinct from this approach, DSM's model aims not so much at rolling up cost, as at evolving an integral budget with a computer program generating the entire expense and revenue pattern from primary input data. The reduction intended by Du Pont of intermediate and end product cost prices to primary cost elements was nevertheless accomplished as a by-product.

Assumed in the model was a cost-centre hierarchy in which assignment is unidirectional; 'back-assignment' had to be incorporated by an external device. In the early sixties, this was the only feasible method of adapting the job of handling hundreds of cost centres to the computer.

## 5.4. THE GENERAL MODEL

In the previous sections the historical situation from which the DSM model arose was outlined, as an introduction to its more specific treatment in sections 5.5 and 5.6 (first and second phases). As a frame of reference for this treatment, the appendix contains a generalized model, using matrix notation. The differences observed between the two phases can mainly be explained from historical backgrounds (capacity of the computer, user implementation, developments in management reporting, etc.).


5.5. THE FIRST PHASE

As has been said before, models were developed at this stage on the basic assumption that cost centres could be placed on a sequence to make the flow of charges one-way only. Under this assumption, cost centres are connected unidirectionally, in the sense that expenditure rolls from one cost centre into those following, and not the other way round. Back-charging is not done by the model itself, but by a device external to it. In matrix terms, this implies the use of upper-triangular matrices, whose inverses can be easily calculated.

One may ask whether the 'one-way hypothesis' was not too specific. Why not fill up the entire matrix?

It should not be forgotten, however, that the computers in general use at the time were not of a size to invert the large matrices (say, 2000 × 2000) that would have resulted. Of course, it would have been possible to develop a total budget on this principle by the detour of sub-budget runs, but this was felt to have greater drawbacks than the one-way approach.

Secondly, it should be borne in mind that for planners and accountants, accustomed to conventional accounting concepts, the step to matrices is a difficult one. With the more transparent roll-up system in place of matrix inversion, all could develop an understanding of the model. Thus it was achieved that already in this phase the results generated were put to full practical use. As an additional advantage, the output was so structured that the charges to an item were traceable throughout. For many of the users, matrix inversion might have meant a leap into the dark.

On the basis of the one-way hypothesis, DSM could compute for all products and services the variable costs, capacity costs, and allocations, thus developing a fully automated budget for its more than 2000 cost centres, with about 40,000 input items. In fact, the budgeting model comprised two separate computational runs, one evolving the physical flows, the other converting these to cash and performing the allocations. The second run was basically simple, starting from the tape with records presenting at the individual cost centres to be charged the physical flows assigned to them and, at the supplying cost centres, the physical totals they had delivered.

In this way, the entire costing job on the Univac III took about six minutes computing time.

The model described had the following advantages:

- The budgeting function was fully automated by a system that linked up well with the users' prior experience.
- Using the program, the accumulated primary costs could be evolved as a by-product by leaving out in the run all primary cost categories except the one under study, say, depreciations. In this way, the full budget in primary form can be developed repeating the procedure for each of the cost categories involved.
- The same procedure can also be applied to compute not only net, but also gross proceeds (net plus depreciations). In that case, the program is run omitting the cost category depreciations.
- If for short-term decisions one wishes to know the differential cost, only such charges as are fully variable with both departments of origin and destination are included in the run. The result then shows in what way cost is affected by small variations in the volumes produced.
- By substituting investment per cost centre for the primary costs, the same procedure could be used to perform the accumulated capital allocation.

The model outlined above also had a number of obvious drawbacks:

- The flow of charges being basically one-way, an artifice had to be employed to incorporate back-charges. In fact, this was done by entering the back-charges beforehand as guesses, both of quantities and prices, which in cost totalling were absorbed in the prices and rates to be charged. Comprised in the software was an iterative routine which in a few steps adjusted the prices and rates to their correct levels. Nevertheless this procedure was rather awkward for the users, since back-charges had to be especially put in on the basis of prior distribution.
- Similar problems were encountered with certain utilities (e.g. steam), because of the circular processes involved. In these cases, insertion of special features in the program was required.
- The above two problems suggest the use of a sequence code allowing the cost centres in the roll-up procedure to be handled in such order as will involve the fewest possible back-charges. This gives, however, rise to a third difficulty: the user finds himself confronted with cost centres in an arrangement different from the habitual one and inconsistent with existing lines of organization and conventional accounting codes.

## 5.6. THE SECOND PHASE

After several years of successful operation, the program's shortcomings, along with a number of sophistications that had become part of it, made a reappraisal of its basic conception advisable. An in-depth study was undertaken and on the basis of this a new program could be developed when faster hardware with a larger storage capacity (Univac 1108) had become available.

In the new model, the roll-up philosophy has been completely abandoned. The program now develops and solves a large number of equations so as to establish not only the quantitative balances of raw and auxiliary materials, intermediates, and some services, but also the complete cost allocation. The method operates irrespective of cost centre sequence and no special provisions need be made for anomalies in this respect. As distinct from the roll-up method, the new approach does, therefore, not require a rigid coding system for its input, but the usual accounting codes can be employed.

By admitting of a congruous cost centre and cost category classification for the budgeting and the accounting function, the new model, as a chief improvement over its predecessor, provides an integrated management information system, in which the budget input refers to existing master files also used for checking and updating the 'actual' records. The output of the budgeting program is also used for calculating the monthly budget and for comparing budgeted and actual amounts, the variances – both in physical and financial terms – being analyzed in a separate program. Furthermore, it has also been employed as a basis (first year) for medium-term planning.

The program retains a number of theoretical drawbacks. In the case of alternative production routes, for instance, a preference must be stated. In practice, however, this is no great problem, since the economic efficiencies of the individual routes are known.


5.7. CONCLUSIONS WITH RESPECT TO THE IMPLEMENTATION

The budgeting model here described is in company-wide operation within DSM, its level of detail increasing according as it is used for reporting to Corporate Management, or to the management of the various divisions of the enterprise, or for careful monitoring of the cost centres by those immediately responsible for them. Planners at the various levels fully participate in the budgeting process.

There are a few obvious reasons why the model was so successfully implemented. Proper implementation of a fundamentally new concept calls for a phasing-in approach, with ample time for the users to adapt. On the technological level, the pace for this development was set by the evolution in the hardware field.

Thus, helpful factors in the implementation were the following:

- At the formulation stage, the company had long experience with massive (punched-card) data handling, and a reasonable degree of integration of its accounting and financial analysis systems.
- The roll-up model was initiated in one part of the company by involving the budgeting staff who used to do the manual job. Once it was operational there, the colleagues in other parts were soon convinced. Thus the system was allowed to grow from the bottom and was not imposed by some planning department.
- The matrix concept was introduced not before the roll-up method had been successfully operated for some ten years.
- As a major improvement over the roll-up method, the matrix model can operate without a specially designed cost centre sequence, so that it directly links up with the usual accounting code systems. The accumulated primary-cost charging, also, is done more efficiently, since a number of primary-cost categories are accumulated simultaneously.

In the above, an outline description was given of a budgeting model. Emphasis was not so much on technical aspects as on implementation and the various phases through which this progressed. To the theorist the next step is obvious: the model could be built out into a linear program, thus to allow for alternative production routes. The practical man will say: just let the system first become fully established before taking the next step, if that should prove necessary; the opting-out of users is more serious than using a theoretically sub-optimum program.

# APPENDIX 5.1.   Mathematical description of the generalized model

The following model is a generalized description of the DSM budgeting model, a mathematical formalization being used for a more succinct treatment.

In producing their software, DSM have, in many cases where this could afford a more streamlined program, taken avail of the properties of certain matrices (e.g. of triangular matrices where no back-deliveries occurred).

After describing the general model (1), we shall give a numerical example (2).

## 1. THE GENERAL MODEL

### a. Diagram of the relationships among the elements of the model

The model comprises such elements as the cost centres (general services, departments manufacturing intermediate and final products), the primary inputs (raw materials and capacity costs), and final output (sales on the market). Relationships among these are shown in table 5.1.

### b. Definitions and symbols

This model is based on the data of the budget and the relations of the departments and the products. The ultimate result is the calculated profit of the end products.

The data are (see table 5.2 for the example)[2].

$A$    matrix of the charging rates
$L$    matrix of the capacity costs
$R$    matrix of technical coefficients, i.e. the elements of the matrix give the amount of input per unit of output
$f$    vector of the final output quantities
$p$    vector of the prices

The other symbols are:

$B$    matrix of the direct and indirect capacity costs of the intermediate products
$C$    matrix of the charged capacity costs of the general services

*Table 5.1.*   Relationships among the elements of the model.

| to<br>from | general<br>services<br>(i) | intermediate<br>products<br>(m) | end<br>products<br>(k) | final<br>output | total |
|---|---|---|---|---|---|
| general<br>services<br>(i) | | | | | |
| interme-<br>diate<br>products<br>(m) | | $E_{mm}$ | $E_{mk}$ | $f_m$ | $q_m$ |
| end<br>products<br>(k) | | | $E_{kk}$ | $e_k$ | $f_k$ | $q_k$ |
| raw<br>materials<br>(s) | | $E_{sm}$ | $E_{sk}$ | | $q_s$ |
| capacity<br>costs<br>(t) | $L_{ti}$ | $L_{tm}$ | $L_{tk}$ | | |
| total | | | | | |

⊠ : box is empty; no relationship exists.

$E$   matrix of total deliveries
$K$   matrix of total costs
$V$   matrix of variable costs
$X$   matrix of the accumulated costs of intermediate products
$e$   vector of total deliveries
$k$   vector of costs
$q$   vector of production quantities
$s$   vector of direct costs
$w$   vector of profits

The subscripts of the matrices and vectors indicate the dimensional range of the matrix (vector). The subscripts are:

$i$   number of general services
$m$   number of intermediate products
$k$   number of end products
$s$   number of raw materials
$t$   number of capacity costs

Hence, for example:

$A_{im}$   matrix of charging rates for general services ($i$) to intermediate products ($m$)
$E_{mk}$   matrix of total deliveries from the intermediate products ($m$) to the end products ($k$)
$R_{mm}$   the internal technical coefficients of the intermediate products ($m$)
$C_{tk}$   matrix of the charged costs ($t$) of the general services to the end products ($k$)

## c. The model

### c.1. The calculation of the variable costs

If the vector $f_k$ of the final output of end products, as well as the matrix $R_{kk}$ of the amount of end product required per unit of end product[3] are given, then the total number $q_k$ of units of end product to be manufactured can be calculated from:

$$q_k = f_k + R_{kk}f_k + R_{kk}^2 f_k + \ldots$$
$$= (I - R_{kk})^{-1} f_k \qquad (5.1)$$

The matrix $E_{mk}$ of the total deliveries of $m$ intermediate products to $k$ end products can be calculated from:

$$E_{mk} = R_{mk} \hat{Q}_{kk} \qquad (5.2)$$

i.e. the intermediate-product volume absorbed in the end products equals the per-unit requirement $(R_{mk})$ multiplied by the total units of end product manufactured[2] $(\hat{Q}_{kk})$.

The total end product volume $(\hat{Q}_{kk})$ can be divided into the final output $(\hat{F}_{kk})$ and the internal deliveries $(E_{kk})$. The latter can also be calculated as a matrix from:

$$E_{kk} = \{(I - R_{kk})^{-1} - I\} \hat{F}_{kk} \qquad (5.3)$$

Let $f_m$ be the vector of deliveries from intermediate to end products:[4]

$$f_m = E_{mk} 1_k \qquad (5.4)$$

then the total volume $q_m$ of intermediate products manufactured is:

$$q_m = (I - R_{mm})^{-1} f_m \qquad (5.5)$$

and the matrix of internal deliveries of intermediate products:

$$E_{mm} = \{(I - R_{mm})^{-1} - I\} \hat{F}_{mm} \qquad (5.6)$$

At the same time, for the matrices of the raw-material deliveries we have:

$$E_{sm} = R_{sm} \hat{Q}_{mm} \qquad (5.7)$$

$$E_{sk} = R_{sk} \hat{Q}_{kk} \qquad (5.8)$$

The matrices of the variable costs (raw-material costs) $(V)$ are the products of prices $(p)$ and deliveries $(E)$:

$$V_{sm} = \hat{P}_{ss} E_{sm} \qquad (5.9)$$

$$V_{sk} = \hat{P}_{ss} E_{sk} \qquad (5.10)$$

(see table 5.3 of the numerical example).

c.2. Allocation of the costs of general services
The accumulated costs $C_{ti}$ of the general services can be written as:

$$\begin{aligned} C_{ti} &= L_{ti} + L_{ti} A_{ii} + L_{ti} A_{ii}^2 + \ldots \\ &= L_{ti} (I - A_{ii})^{-1} \end{aligned} \qquad (5.11)$$

Hence, the general-service costs charged to the intermediate products as a product of the costs and the charging rates

$$C_{tm} = C_{ti} A_{im} \tag{5.12}$$

and for end products:

$$C_{tk} = C_{ti} A_{ik} \tag{5.13}$$

(see table 5.4).

### c.3. The costs of the intermediate products
The total capacity costs $B_{tm}$ of the intermediate products are the capacity costs charged to them by the general services plus their own capacity costs:

$$B_{tm} = C_{tm} + L_{tm} \tag{5.14}$$

Between intermediate products deliveries also occur. For a correct allocation, direct costs must be multiplied by the accumulated coefficients, in a similar fashion to equation (5.11), in order to calculate the accumulated costs of the intermediate products $(X_{s+t,m})$.

The charging rates[5] can be calculated as the ratio of the deliveries between intermediate products $(E_{mm})$ and the total volume of products $(q_m)$:

$$A_{mm} = E_{mm} \hat{Q}_{mm}^{-1} \tag{5.15}$$

The accumulated costs are:

$$X_{s+t,m} = \begin{bmatrix} V_{sm} \\ B_{tm} \end{bmatrix} [I - A_{mm}]^{-1} \tag{5.16}$$

The total costs of the intermediate products $(k_m)$ are:

$$k'_m = 1'_{s+t} X_{s+t,m} \tag{5.17}$$

### c.4. The profit of the end products
The transfer price $(p_m)$[6] of the intermediate products is the ratio of the total costs and the total volume of intermediate products, or

$$\hat{P}_{mm} = \hat{K}_{mm} \hat{Q}_{mm}^{-1} \tag{5.18}$$

The costs of the deliveries of intermediate products to end products $(K_{mk})$ are:

$$K_{mk} = \hat{P}_{mm} E_{mk} \tag{5.19}$$

The direct costs of the end products $(s_k)$ are

$$s'_k = 1'_s V_{sk} + 1'_t L_{tk} + 1'_t C_{tk} + 1'_m K_{mk} \tag{5.20}$$

Between end products deliveries also occur $(E_{kk})$, which are charged at market prices $(p_k)$. The total costs $k_k$ of the end products are:

$$k'_k = s'_k + 1'_k (E'_{kk} \hat{P}_{kk}) - 1'_k (E'_{kk} \hat{P}_{kk})' \tag{5.21}$$

The profit on the end products can now be defined as the revenues of the end products minus the total costs:

$$w'_k = f'_k \hat{P}_{kk} - k'_k \tag{5.22}$$

## 2. NUMERICAL EXAMPLE

In table 5.2 the required data for the budget are collected:

- the volumes demanded of the $k$ end products and their market prices ($f_k$ and $p_k$ vectors)
- the technical coefficients, i.e. the per-unit input of the $m$ intermediate products, $k$ end products, and $s$ raw materials ($R$ matrices)
- the prices of the $s$ raw materials ($p_s$ vector)
- the capacity costs, particularly wages and depreciations ($L$ matrices)
- the charging rates of general-service costs to general services, intermediate products and end products ($A$ matrices).

In this example we have four general services, three intermediate products and six end products.

The capacity costs are wages, depreciation of buildings and depreciation of machinery.

With these data the total model of section 5.1 is checked. In table 5.3 are given the results after equation (5.10) and in table 5.4 those after equation (5.13).

Equation (5.17) is: $k'_m = k'_3 = \begin{bmatrix} 2033 & 1587 & 2915 \end{bmatrix}$.

The internal prices of the intermediate products are (equation (5.18)) $\begin{bmatrix} 135.5 & 63.5 & 9.7 \end{bmatrix}$. In table 5.5 the total result is given.

Table 5.2. Basic data.

| | General services (i) | | | | Intermediate products (m) | | | End products (k) | | | | | | Price per unit |
|---|---|---|---|---|---|---|---|---|---|---|---|---|---|---|
| | General management | Maintenance | Techn. services | Design department | a | b | c | A | B | C | D | $E_1$ | $E_2$ | $p_s$ |
| | | | | | **Technical coefficients per unit output** | | | | | | | | | |
| | | | | | $R_{mm}$ | | | $R_{mk}$ | | | | | | |
| Intermediate product a | | | | | | | $\frac{1}{60}$ | 1.0 | | | | $\frac{1}{160}$ | 0.01 | |
| Intermediate product b | | | | | | | | | 1.0 | | | $\frac{1}{40}$ | | |
| Intermediate product c | | | | | | | | | | | | | | |
| Product $E_1$ | | | | | | | | | | | | | 0.01* | |
| | | | | | $R_{sm}$ | | | $R_{sk}$ | | | | | | |
| Material 1 | | | | | 4.0 | | | | 0.15 | | 0.1 | $\frac{1}{80}$ | | 4.00 |
| Material 2 | | | | | | | | 0.1 | | 0.25 | | | 0.1 | 2.00 |
| Material 3 | | | | | $\frac{20}{3}$ | | 0.2 | | | 0.25 | | $\frac{3}{80}$ | | 8.00 |
| Material 4 | | | | | | | 0.4 | -0.1 | | | 0.5 | | | 2.00 |
| Material 5 | | | | | | | | | | | -0.1 | | | 1.00 |
| Material 6 | | | | | 2.0 | | | | -0.1 | | -0.1 | | | 1.00 |
| Material 7 | | | | | | 2.0 | | 0.2 | 0.5 | 1.0 | | 0.5 | | 0.50 |
| Material 8 | | | | | | 1.0 | | 0.5 | | | 0.2 | | 0.2 | 0.20 |
| Material 9 | | | | | | | | | | 2.0 | | | 0.5 | 3.00 |
| Material 10 | | | | | 0.2 | | | | | | 0.4 | | | 7.00 |

**Prices and quantities of the end products**

Products ($k$):

| | $k_1$ | $k_2$ | $k_3$ | $k_4$ | $k_5$ | $k_6$ |
|---|---|---|---|---|---|---|
| Prices $p'_k$ | 15 | 21.25 | 37.50 | 10 | 7.50 | 10 |
| Quantity $f_k$ | 100 | 200 | 200 | 1000 | 790 | 1000 |

Primary costs and charging rates:

| | Service departments ($i$) — $L_{ti}$ / $A_{ii}$ | | | | Main departments ($m$) — $L_{tm}$ (Capacity costs) / $A_{im}$ | | | | | End products ($k$) — $L_{tk}$ / $A_{ik}$ ($f_k$) | | | | | |
|---|---|---|---|---|---|---|---|---|---|---|---|---|---|---|---|
| | GM | Maint. | T.s. | Des. | $m_1$ | $m_2$ | $m_3$ | $m_4$ | $m_5$ | $k_1$ | $k_2$ | $k_3$ | $k_4$ | $k_5$ | $k_6$ |
| Wages | 1500 | 600 | 550 | | 1100 | 600 | 600 | 500 | 680 | 500 | 2000 | 2100 | 3700 | 1100 | 3000 |
| Depreciation of buildings | 100 | 100 | 50 | | 100 | 300 | 200 | 500 | 500 | 500 | 100 | 2000 | 300 | 200 | 1000 |
| Depreciation of machinery | 50 | | 50 | | 50 | 100 | 200 | 500 | 500 | 500 | 400 | 900 | 1000 | 700 | 500 |
| General management | 0.05 | 0.05 | | | 0.1 | 0.1 | 0.1 | 0.1 | 0.1 | 0.1 | 0.1 | 0.1 | 0.1 | 0.05 | 0.05 |
| Maintenance | 0.1 | 0.1 | | | 0.1 | 0.1 | 0.1 | 0.1 | 0.1 | 0.1 | 0.1 | 0.1 | 0.1 | 0.05 | 0.05 |
| Techn. serv. | 0.1 | | | | | | | | | | 0.1 | 0.1 | 0.4 | 0.2 | 0.2 |
| Design dept. | | | | | 0.2 | 0.2 | 0.2 | 0.2 | 0.2 | 0.2 | 0.2 | | | | |

\* The elements of $R_{kk}$ are 0, except for $R_{56} = 0.01$.

*Table 5.3.* Primary costs.

| | General management | Maintenance | Techn. serv. | Design dept. | a | b | c | A | B | C | D | E₁ | E₂ | Total |
|---|---|---|---|---|---|---|---|---|---|---|---|---|---|---|
| Units of products (internal + external) | | | | | 15 | 25 | 300 | 100 | 200 | 200 | 1000 | 800 | 1000 | |
| Material 1 | | | | | 240 | | | | 120 | | 400 | 40 | | 800 |
| Material 2 | | | | | | | 120 | | | 100 | | | 200 | 420 |
| Material 3 | | | | | | | 240 | 80 | | 400 | | | | 720 |
| Material 4 | | | | | 200 | | | | | | 1000 | 240 | | 1440 |
| Material 5 | | | | | | | | −10 | | | −100 | | | −110 |
| Material 6 | | | | | | | | | −20 | | −100 | | | −120 |
| Material 7 | | | | | 15 | 25 | | 10 | 50 | 100 | | 200 | 100 | 500 |
| Material 8 | | | | | | 5 | | 10 | | | 40 | | | 55 |
| Material 9 | | | | | | | | | | 1200 | | | 1500 | 2700 |
| Material 10 | | | | | 21 | | | | | | 2800 | | | 2821 |
| Wages | 1500 | 600 | 550 | 1100 | 600 | 600 | 680 | 500 | 2000 | 2100 | 3700 | 1100 | 3000 | 18030 |
| Depr. build. | 100 | 100 | 50 | 100 | 300 | 200 | 500 | 500 | 100 | 2000 | 300 | 200 | 1000 | 5450 |
| Depr. mach. | 50 | | | 50 | 100 | 200 | 500 | 500 | 400 | 900 | 1000 | 700 | 500 | 4900 |
| Total of primary costs | 1650 | 700 | 600 | 1250 | 1476 | 1030 | 2040 | 1590 | 2650 | 6800 | 9040 | 2480 | 6300 | 37606 |

## Table 5.4. Costs after allocation of general services costs.

| | a | b | c | A | B | C | D | E$_1$ | E$_2$ | Total |
|---|---|---|---|---|---|---|---|---|---|---|
| Material 1 | 240 | | | | 120 | | 400 | 40 | | 800 |
| Material 2 | | 120 | | | | 100 | | | 200 | 420 |
| Material 3 | | | | 80 | | 400 | | 240 | | 720 |
| Material 4 | 200 | | 240 | | | | 1000 | | | 1440 |
| Material 5 | | | | −10 | | | −100 | | | −110 |
| Material 6 | | | | | −20 | | −100 | | | −120 |
| Material 7 | 15 | 25 | | 10 | 50 | 100 | | 200 | 100 | 500 |
| Material 8 | | 5 | | 10 | | | 40 | | | 55 |
| Material 9 | | | | | | 1200 | | | 1500 | 2700 |
| Material 10 | 21 | | | | | | 2800 | | | 2821 |
| Wages | 600 | 600 | 680 | 500 | 2000 | 2100 | 3700 | 1100 | 3000 | 14280 |
| Depr. build. | 300 | 200 | 500 | 500 | 100 | 2000 | 300 | 200 | 1000 | 5100 |
| Depr. mach. | 100 | 200 | 500 | 500 | 400 | 900 | 1000 | 700 | 500 | 4800 |
| Allocated costs of | | | | | | | | | | |
| Wages | 495 | 495 | 495 | 495 | 495 | 287 | 494 | 247 | 247 | 3750 |
| Depr. build. | 46 | 46 | 46 | 46 | 46 | 27 | 47 | 23 | 23 | 350 |
| Depr. mach. | 16 | 16 | 16 | 16 | 16 | 6 | 6 | 4 | 4 | 100 |
| Total | 2033 | 1587 | 2597 | 2147 | 3207 | 7120 | 9587 | 2754 | 6574 | 37606 |

## Table 5.5. Revenues, costs, and profits of the end products.

| | A | B | C | D | E$_1$ | E$_2$ | Total |
|---|---|---|---|---|---|---|---|
| Primary costs: | | | | | | | |
| Material 1 | | 120 | | 400 | 40 | | 560 |
| Material 2 | | | 100 | | | 200 | 300 |
| Material 3 | 80 | | 400 | | 240 | | 720 |
| Material 4 | | | | 1000 | | | 1000 |
| Material 5 | −10 | | | −100 | | | −110 |
| Material 6 | | −20 | | −100 | | | −120 |
| Material 7 | 10 | 50 | 100 | | 200 | 100 | 460 |
| Material 8 | 10 | | | 40 | | | 50 |
| Material 9 | | | 1200 | | | 1500 | 2700 |
| Material 10 | | | | 2800 | | | 2800 |
| Wages | 500 | 2000 | 2100 | 3700 | 1100 | 3000 | 12400 |
| Depr. of buildings | 500 | 100 | 2000 | 300 | 200 | 1000 | 4100 |
| Depr. of machines | 500 | 400 | 900 | 1000 | 700 | 500 | 4000 |
| Allocated costs: | | | | | | | |
| wages of gen. departments | 495 | 495 | 287 | 494 | 247 | 247 | 2265 |
| depr. of build. of departments | 46 | 46 | 27 | 47 | 23 | 23 | 212 |
| depr. of mach. of departments | 16 | 16 | 6 | 6 | 4 | 4 | 52 |
| costs of a | | | | | 677 | 1355 | 2032 |
| costs of b | | | | | 1270 | | 1270 |
| costs of c | 972 | 1943 | | | | | 2915 |
| $s_k^l$ (equation 5.20) | 3119 | 5150 | 7120 | 9587 | 4701 | 7929 | 37606 |
| Internal deliveries | | | | | −75 | 75 | |
| Total costs | 3119 | 5150 | 7120 | 9587 | 4626 | 8004 | 37606 |
| Revenues | 1500 | 4250 | 7500 | 10000 | 5925 | 10000 | 39175 |
| Profit | −1619 | −900 | +380 | +413 | +1299 | +1996 | 1569 |

NOTES

1. R. L. Hershey and C. R. Schwartz, 'Computers in management cost accounting', *Chemical Engineering Progress* 53(1957), 333–337.
2. Capitals represent matrices, lower case letters vectors, whilst the symbol ^ indicates a diagonal matrix with the vector components as the diagonal elements.
3. End products are marketable products, but may also be absorbed in other end products.
4. $1_k$ = vector, having $k$ components of 1.
5. The charging rates of the general services are given. The rates of the intermediate products are based on real deliveries (equation 5.15).
6. The price vectors are given except the transfer prices (equation 5.18).

# 6. Cost accounting, planning and budgeting

A. BOSMAN and J. L. BOUMA

In the literature of managerial economics several definitions of the notions of plan and budget and also divergent opinions of the relations between these notions are found. A *plan* can be conceived as a decision or a set of connected decisions about a line of conduct to be followed, taking into account the alternatives from which to choose, the objectives, and the restrictions under which the activities must be performed. A plan can be set up according to several methods and techniques. There are simple methods in which desired value(s) of one or more endogenous variables (e.g., sales) and/or desired situations (e.g., the financial structure) are fixed normatively, the remaining activities (e.g., the volume of production and the level of stocks and investments) being adapted to them consistently or not. There are mathematically complex methods by which the solution of the planning problem can be formalized. Especially if, as in an organization, the implementation of a plan requires the cooperation of several individuals or groups of individuals, the plan must be so specified that every person concerned can read from it what he is expected to do in order that the total activities shall be executed co-ordinatedly.

The *budget* can be seen as a special manifestation of a plan: namely, as a specification of that plan in a form which corresponds with the financial accounting reports. In this form the plan is translated into a set of quantitatively formulated tasks and authorizations for the budgetees. The budget control ensures that the execution of the plan, as the plan itself, is represented in quantitative factors (and relations) which are often expressed in monetary units. *Financial accounting* is based for an important part on cost accounting. Historically cost control procedures form a large portion of budget control. So it is in line with history to relate budgeting and planning to cost accounting. It will especially be shown that the standard costing procedures, in which the interdepartmental transactions are specified as to their financial consequences for the final products, show a structure which, in some ways, corresponds with the structure of a linear programming model. This similarity offers possibilities of straightening out certain imperfections in the costing procedures. This 'face lifting' has consequences for the meaning of costing and of budgeting.

## 6.1. COST FUNCTIONS AND PRODUCT COSTING

Decision making in relation to the 'what', 'how much' and 'how' of the input of means of production in an organization requires knowledge of the rewards and costs connected with the several alternatives of the input. The knowledge about the relation between the input of means of production and their costs is sometimes expressed in a cost function. In a cost function the input of the means of production (expressed in quantities of physical units, or in (equivalent) quantities of monetary units) is related to the quantities of the respective products produced during the period considered. While defining cost functions, sometimes exogenous variables are used that define the character of the production process. Examples of these variables are lot size of production, number of machine set-ups and number of failures of various kinds.

The construction of cost functions can take place in several ways. In the first place the definition of the cost function by means of *statistical methods*, especially the correlation and regression analysis, can be mentioned. In the literature several good results of these methods are known[1]. A second category of methods for the construction of cost functions is known by the name of *standard cost accounting*. This method has, contrary to correlation analysis, the property of strongly positing relations through systematic deduction from a set of axiomatic principles, to which e.g. the matching principle belongs. This principle has been interpreted by many authors as one of causality which is elaborated as follows. Every production and every product causes costs. The quantitative effect of the causal relations between costs on the one hand and a specific quantity of product on the other is expressed in a standard quantity. The *standard cost* of a certain product is dependent on several factors such as the composition of the assortment (defined as the vector of the quantities of the several products produced during the time period considered), the production methods, and the prices of the means of production. About each of these factors a normative statement has to be made before one can proceed to the calculation of costs. We shall return to the normative meaning of these assumptions later on in this article. Through these normative statements a number of starting points are standardized in relation to the production process. Starting from standardized factors, one tries to make a point estimate of the relation between the total costs and the total quantities of the products in the assortment. While elaborating this concept it is assumed that the input of a certain means of production $i$ in behalf of the production of one unit of product $j$ can be expressed as a constant standard-technical relation through a so-called technical coefficient $a_{ij}$. The matching principle is interpreted as a constant causal relation between the input of the means of production and the number of units of a homogeneous product:

$$b_{ij} = a_{ij} \cdot g_j \tag{6.1}$$

$b_{ij}$ = the standard input of a means of production $i$ on behalf of the production of the quantity $g_j$ of the product $j$

$g_j$ = the standard quantity of product $j$ during a unit of time

$a_{ij}$ = the standard technical coefficient of a given production method

$i$ = 1, 2, 3, ..., $r$

$j$ = 1, 2, 3, ..., $s$

In principle, the technical coefficients are taken from technological research[2]. If the production technique and the efficiency of production are dependent on human interference, the determination of the technical coefficients is based on 'normal' diligence and motivation of the workers. In that case the coefficients may have a normative character.

We define the matrix of the technical coefficients as:

$$A = \begin{bmatrix} a_{11} & a_{12} & a_{13} & \cdots & a_{1s} \\ a_{21} & a_{22} & a_{23} & \cdots & a_{2s} \\ \vdots & \vdots & \vdots & & \vdots \\ a_{r1} & a_{r2} & a_{r3} & \cdots & a_{rs} \end{bmatrix}$$

Given the vector of the quantities of products (per period)

$$g = \begin{bmatrix} g_1 \\ g_2 \\ g_3 \\ \vdots \\ g_s \end{bmatrix}$$

a diagonal matrix $\hat{G}$ can be defined, in which the elements on the main diagonal are equal to the corresponding elements of the vector $g$. Next we define a matrix $B$ as

$$B = \begin{bmatrix} b_{11} & b_{12} & b_{13} & \cdots & b_{1s} \\ b_{21} & b_{22} & b_{23} & \cdots & b_{2s} \\ \vdots & \vdots & \vdots & & \vdots \\ b_{r1} & b_{r2} & b_{r3} & \cdots & b_{rs} \end{bmatrix}$$

According to equation (6.1)

$$B = A \cdot \hat{G} \tag{6.2}$$

For any means of production $i$ the total can be defined as

$$b_i = \sum_{j=1}^{s} b_{ij} = \sum_{j=1}^{s} a_{ij} \cdot g_j \tag{6.3}$$

Vector $b$ is defined as:

$$b = \begin{bmatrix} b_1 \\ b_2 \\ b_3 \\ \vdots \\ b_r \end{bmatrix} = A \cdot g \tag{6.4}$$

Vector $b$ gives a general view of the physical costs connected with $g$, classified by kinds of costs. The relations (6.3) and (6.4) are to be taken as physical cost functions.

In general, it is possible to express the physical costs, $b_i$, in an equivalent amount of monetary costs, $k_i$. This can be done by multiplying the quantity $b_i$ by a price per unit, $p_i$ (the variable $p_i$ has been expressed as a number of monetary units per unit of the means of production $i$). Under certain conditions it is relevant to define $p_i$ as the price for which the means of production concerned can be bought on the market. For the present we assume that these conditions for the relevance of the price on the buying market (in contrast with the selling prices on second-hand markets which constitute the opportunity cost) are fulfilled. The value of $p_i$ can be used (possibly with correction for transport and transaction costs) if and as far as the unit of measure in which the means of production concerned is bought on the market (the unit of goods for which the price is quoted) corresponds with the unit of goods in which $b_i$ has been expressed. This applies e.g. to raw materials for which the market prices are specified in the same units as the input of the means of production in the production processes. The relation between $p_i$ and the price on the buying market is more complicated if the purchase of the means of production takes place in different units from those in which the input of the production process (the numerator of the technical coefficients) concerned has been expressed. This complication occurs for example with machines and buildings (defined as durable means of production). The purchase price is expressed as a number of monetary units per machine or per building respectively. The input in the production process is measured in 'units of performance' or 'units of capacity', such as the number of machine-hours, the number of square metres of floor surface per unit of time, or cubic metres of space per unit of time. When a machine has been purchased, it can supply productive performances for several periods of time and in different quantities.

Several questions arise as regards the allocation of the purchase price to the separate units of performance of the durable means of production.

1. How are the purchase costs spread over the separate production periods? (The depreciation problem).
2. Over how many units of performance per production period is the depreciation imputed to that period spread? (The overhead allocation problem).

More than one solution to the depreciation problem is possible. The determination of the depreciations per period requires complementary axioms and conventions[3]. The 'divisor' of the overhead costs per period can be defined as the maximum available quantity (technically speaking) of units of performance of the relevant durable means of production during the period considered (the maximum technical occupation (usage) of the capacity), or as the economically optimum usage of the capacity (also denoted as the normal usage of capacity). This normal usage of capacity is seen in the literature about the standard costs accounting as a particularly relevant basis for allocating the overhead costs and, therefore, for calculating the value of $p_i$ for the input of the services of the durable means of production. Naturally, the investment policy of the company must be focused on maintaining long-term equilibrium between the technically maximum and economically optimum capacity of the durable means of production. Meanwhile it is worth noting that in standard costs accounting an exact quantitative and operational definition of the concept of normal usage of capacities is not generally available. We shall show in this article how a quantitative definition of the term normal usage of capacity with the help of a linear programming model can be given.

In general the following relations hold:

$$k_i = p_i \cdot b_i$$
$$(i = 1, 2, 3, \ldots, r) \qquad (6.5)$$
$$k_{ij} = p_i \cdot b_{ij}$$

In principle, standard costs accounting consists in allocating the total costs, classified in relation to some characteristics of the means of production

$$k = \begin{bmatrix} k_1 \\ k_2 \\ k_3 \\ \vdots \\ k_r \end{bmatrix}$$

to the final products in an acceptable way. The quantities of these products are specified in $g$. For that purpose the total costs per cost classification are spread over the different kinds of products according to:

$$k_{ij} = \frac{p_i \cdot b_{ij} \cdot k_i}{p_i \cdot b_i} = \frac{b_{ij}}{b_i} \cdot k_i \qquad (6.6)$$

Next, the total costs per product $j$ due to the direct input of means of production are calculated,

$$U_j = \sum_{i=1}^{r} k_{ij} \qquad (6.7)$$

The average costs per unit of product $j$ are

$$\overline{U}_j = \frac{U_j}{g_j} \qquad (6.8)$$

The values $b_{ij}$ and $b_i$ are connected with $g$ and $A$ through the equations (6.1) and (6.3). Essentially the problem of the costs allocation boils down to the definition of the matrix $A$. However, before one can define the matrix $A$, a number of problems must be solved. We mention the two major ones.

1. In the process of production a number of intermediate products or services are produced. These intermediate products are produced because they are necessary parts of the final products. The quantities defined in $g$ are those of the intermediate products and the final products. That means $\overline{U}_j$ defines the average costs of the intermediate products or the final products. As we suppose that the intermediate products are not sold, the costs of these intermediate products must be allocated to the final products to permit the calculation of the total costs per unit of these products. To specify relations for this allocation we make use of the concept production centre. A *production centre* is a production

function or a set of production functions defining the relation between
the input of the means of production and the output of an intermediate
product or a final product.

2. A second complication arises from the fact that economically homogeneous products can be obtained according to different ways of production. It is possible to define different production functions having a
qualitatively identical output of economically homogeneous intermediate or final products. We call the various units of a product economically homogeneous if there are no differences between the final products when they are sold on the market, or between the intermediate
products when they are used in the production process. The availability
of several (plural) production possibilities per production centre gives
rise to the problem of the choice of the optimal production method(s).


6.2. THE RELATIONS BETWEEN PRODUCTION CENTRES

In order to specify the procedure for the allocation of the costs of the intermediate products we define a matrix $C$. The element $c_{hj}$ represents the
quantity of the intermediate product $h$ used for the production of one
unit of the intermediate or final product $j$. So the elements of $C$ can be
understood as technical coefficients, which, in contrast with elements
from matrix $A$, in which the input of the means of production is defined,
relate to the use of the intermediate products manufactured by the organization itself. We assume that the intermediate products are not sold
outside the organization and that a production centre does not use self-
manufactured units (i.e., $c_{hj} = 0$ for $h = j$). Besides, we assume that there
are no deliveries of products between the production centres of the final
products. Final products are only sold outside the organization ($c_{hj} = 0$
for all values of $h$, which relate to final products). On account of this
classification the vector $g$ can be subdivided into two subvectors. One
is the subvector of the quantities of the intermediate products ($g_1, g_2, g_3,$
$\ldots, g_t$) and one is the subvector of the quantities of final products ($g_{t+1},$
$g_{t+2}, g_{t+3}, \ldots, g_s$), $t < s$. So $t$ kinds of intermediate products and $s - t$ kinds
of final products are distinguished[4]. Given the classification in intermediate
and final products and the assumptions made, the following equations
apply. For $h = 1, 2, 3, \ldots, t$:

$$g_h = \sum_{j=1}^{s} c_{hj} \cdot g_j \text{ in which } c_{hj} = 0 \text{ for } h = j[5] \tag{6.9}$$

that is to say the produced quantity of intermediate product $h$ is spread
wholly over the production of other intermediate and final products. If

$h = t + 1, t + 2, t + 3, \ldots, s:$

$$c_{hj} = 0 \qquad (6.10)$$

which means that there are no internal deliveries of final products. According to (6.10) the final $s - t$ rows of the matrix $C$ only contain zero elements.

We now define the matrix $D$ as:

$$D = C \cdot \hat{G} \qquad (6.11)$$

The matrix $D$ gives a general view of the internal deliveries in numbers of physical units.

$$
D = \begin{array}{l} \\ \\ \\ \\ \\ \\ \\ \\ s-t \\ \text{rows} \\ \\ \end{array}
\left[
\begin{array}{ccccc|ccc}
0 & c_{12}g_2 & c_{13}g_3 & \cdots & c_{1t}g_t & c_{1,t+1}g_{t+1} & \cdots & c_{1s}g_s \\
c_{21}g_1 & 0 & c_{23}g_3 & \cdots & c_{2t}g_t & c_{2,t+1}g_{t+1} & \cdots & c_{2s}g_s \\
c_{31}g_1 & c_{32}g_2 & 0 & \cdots & c_{3t}g_t & c_{3,t+1}g_{t+1} & \cdots & c_{3s}g_s \\
\vdots & \vdots & \vdots & & \vdots & \vdots & & \vdots \\
c_{t1}g_1 & c_{t2}g_2 & c_{t3}g_3 & \cdots & 0 & c_{t,t+1}g_{t+1} & \cdots & c_{ts}g_s \\
0 & 0 & 0 & \cdots & 0 & 0 & \cdots & 0 \\
\vdots & \vdots & \vdots & & \vdots & \vdots & & \vdots \\
0 & 0 & 0 & \cdots & 0 & 0 & \cdots & 0
\end{array}
\right]
$$

$t$ columns (intermediate products)     $s - t$ columns (final products)

In accordance with equation (6.9) the sum of the elements in the first row of $D$ is equal to $g_1$. In general, the sum of the elements of the $h^{th}$ row equals $g_h$:

$$\sum_{j=1}^{s} d_{hj} = g_h \; (h = 1, 2, 3, \ldots, t) \qquad (6.12)$$

where $d_{hj} = c_{hj} \cdot g_j$

In order to consider the effects of the internal deliveries on the calculation of costs, we make a link with equation (6.7). In this equation a definition is given of the costs connected with the production of $g$ due to the direct use of means of production. The amounts $U_j$ can be denoted as the *direct costs* of $g_j$. We now take into account the fact that several intermediate products are being used in other intermediate and in final products. This implies that the direct costs of intermediate products can be seen as *indirect costs* of other intermediate and final products. Generally speaking, the total (direct and indirect) costs of production centre $h(h \leq t)$ are imputed to other production centres according to the relations expressed by the elements in row $h$ of matrix $D$. A portion of the total costs of production centre $h$, viz.,

$$\frac{c_{hj} \cdot g_j}{g_h} = \frac{d_{hj}}{g_h} = f_{hj} \qquad (6.13)$$

is allocated to production centre $j(j \neq h)$, where

$$0 \leq f_{hj} \leq 1 \text{ and } \sum_{j=1}^{s} f_{hj} = 1 \text{ for } h = 1, 2, 3, \dots t,$$

$$f_{hj} = 0 \text{ for } h = t + 1, t + 2, t + 3, \dots, s.$$

We denote the total costs of production centre $j$ by the symbol $W_j$. For the $s$ production centres the following equations can be drawn up.

$$
\begin{aligned}
W_1 &= U_1 + f_{21} \cdot W_2 + f_{31} \cdot W_3 + \; \dots \; + f_{t1} \cdot W_t \\
W_2 &= f_{12} \cdot W_1 + U_2 + f_{32} \cdot W_3 + \; \dots \; + f_{t2} \cdot W_t \\
&\; . \; . \; . \; . \; . \; . \; . \; . \; . \; . \; . \; . \; . \; . \; . \; . \; . \; . \; . \; . \; . \; . \qquad (6.14a) \\
W_t &= f_{1t} \cdot W_1 + f_{2t} \cdot W_2 + f_{3t} \cdot W_3 + \; \dots \; + U_t
\end{aligned}
$$

$$
\begin{aligned}
W_{t+1} &= f_{1,t+1} \cdot W_1 + f_{2,t+1} \cdot W_2 + f_{3,t+1} \cdot W_3 + \; \dots \\
&\quad + f_{t,t+1} \cdot W_t + U_{t+1} \\
W_{t+2} &= f_{1,t+2} \cdot W_1 + f_{2,t+2} \cdot W_2 + f_{3,t+2} \cdot W_3 + \; \dots \qquad (6.14b) \\
&\quad + f_{t,t+2} \cdot W_t + U_{t+2} \\
&\; . \; . \; . \; . \; . \; . \; . \; . \; . \; . \; . \; . \; . \; . \; . \; . \; . \; . \; . \; . \; . \; . \\
W_s &= f_{1s} \cdot W_1 + f_{2s} \cdot W_2 + f_{3s} \cdot W_s + \; \dots \; + f_{ts} \cdot W_t + U_s
\end{aligned}
$$

This scheme of relations can be rewritten as:

$$
\begin{aligned}
U_1 &= W_1 - f_{21} \cdot W_2 - f_{31} \cdot W_3 - \; \dots \; - f_{t1} \cdot W_t \\
U_2 &= -f_{12} \cdot W_1 + W_2 - f_{32} \cdot W_3 - \; \dots \; - f_{t2} \cdot W_t \\
&\; . \; . \; . \; . \; . \; . \; . \; . \; . \; . \; . \; . \; . \; . \; . \; . \; . \; . \; . \; . \\
U_t &= -f_{1t} \cdot W_1 - f_{2t} \cdot W_2 - f_{3t} \cdot W_3 - \; \dots \; + W_t \\
U_{t+1} &= -f_{1,t+1} \cdot W_1 - f_{2,t+1} \cdot W_2 - f_{3,t+1} \cdot W_3 - \; \dots \qquad (6.15) \\
&\quad -f_{t,t+1} \cdot W_t + W_{t+1} \\
U_{t+2} &= -f_{1,t+2} \cdot W_1 - f_{2,t+2} \cdot W_2 - f_{3,t+2} \cdot W_3 - \; \dots \\
&\quad -f_{t,t+2} \cdot W_t + W_{t+2} \\
&\; . \; . \; . \; . \; . \; . \; . \; . \; . \; . \; . \; . \; . \; . \; . \; . \; . \; . \; . \; . \\
U_s &= -f_{1s} \cdot W_1 - f_{2s} \cdot W_2 - f_{3s} \cdot W_3 - \; \dots \; - f_{ts} \cdot W_t + W_s
\end{aligned}
$$

In matrix notation, (6.15) can be written as:

$$U = (E - F') \cdot W \tag{6.16}$$

$U$ = the vector of the direct costs
$W$ = the vector of the total costs per production centre
$E$ = the identity matrix of the order $s \times s$
$F'$ = the transpose of matrix $F$, the characteristic element of which is defined in equation (6.13).

If the equations (6.15) are independent and the matrix $E - F'$ is non-singular, then (6.16) can be rewritten as:

$$W = (E - F')^{-1} \cdot U \tag{6.17}$$

Given $g$, the cost price of the final products can be calculated[6,7].

## 6.3. ALTERNATIVE PRODUCTION METHODS OF ECONOMICALLY HOMOGENEOUS PRODUCTS

From the previous general view of the standard cost accounting procedure one can learn that the allocation of costs is based on data of different kinds. Partly they are exogenous variables, such as purchase prices of means of production and technical coefficients (at a given degree of efficiency of the production process). Partly they are variables that are fixed through a decision of the management of the organization, such as the quantities $g$ that must be produced. Essentially the specification of matrices $A$ and $C$ (and derived matrices) is also the result of a decision, which concerns not so much the technical coefficients per production function (in l.p. literature called activity), but the choice of the relevant columns expressing the production functions considered or actually used. When the producer has a multiple choice (in the case of economically homogeneous products), the question arises which production function or combination of production functions is selected from the matrices $A$ and $C$. Some authors contend that this should be the production function incurring the lowest cost prices for a given vector $g$. Others let the choice depend on the availability of the means of production and a priori leave all possibilities open. However, they will also have to make some kind of decision regarding the production functions, otherwise it is impossible to specify the matrices $A$ and $C$ (see the preceding sections).

We shall now pay attention to the way in which the plural production technique per product can be expressed in a model in order to find the connection with the planning model to be discussed below. Therefore we maintain the distinction previously made between intermediate and final products, as well as the assumptions made with regard to matrix $C$. In relation to the intermediate products the following can be observed. For the technically different variants of economically homogeneous inter- mediate products separate elements are specified in vector $g$. In the matrices $A$ and $C$ separate columns are specified for each of the possible production functions of a production centre. If we want to keep matrix $C$ square, the same number of rows must be added as that of additional columns. The presence of these extra rows leads to an incorrect specifica- tion of the planning model. We will explain this by an example. According to equation (6.9) we have

$$C \cdot g = \begin{bmatrix} g_1 \\ g_2 \\ g_3 \\ \vdots \\ g_t \\ 0 \\ 0 \\ \vdots \\ 0 \end{bmatrix} \Big\} s - t \text{ elements} \qquad (6.18)$$

We suppose that intermediate products 1, 2, and 3 are economically homo- geneous. Equation (6.18) expresses that for the production of goods 4, 5, 6, ..., $s$ use is made of intermediate product 1 according to the first row of $C$, of intermediate product 2 according to the second row of $C$, and of intermediate product 3 according to the third row. The input according to rows 1, 2 and 3 of $C$ is represented *additively* instead of, as it should be in the planning model, *alternatively*. Hence, for the sake of the relevance of the model it is necessary to replace the output according to the three equations:

$$\sum_{j=1}^{s} c_{1j} \cdot g_j = g_1$$

$\qquad$ *plus*

$$\sum_{j=1}^{s} c_{2j} \cdot g_j = g_2 \qquad (6.19)$$

*plus*

$$\sum_{j=1}^{s} c_{3j} \cdot g_j = g_3$$

(where $c_{ij} = 0$, $i, j = 1, \ldots, 3$)

by one equation, in which the output is defined as:

$$\sum_{j=1}^{s} c_{(1, 2, 3)j} \cdot g_j = g_1 + g_2 + g_3 \qquad (6.20)$$

This substitution means that matrix $C$ is reduced to a matrix $_rC$ by leaving only *one* of each collection of identical rows in $C$. Moreover, we delete in $_rC$ the last $s$ rows, so that $_rC$ only contains rows that specify the relations between the production centres delivering the intermediate products and the production centres receiving them. The order of $_rC$ is $(t \times s)$. We now define a matrix $EE$ of the same order as $_rC$, by replacing in the identity matrix $E$ of the order $(s \times s)$ some zeroes by ones in the row for each production centre representing more than one production function, and by deleting all the rows of the production centre producing final products. The element 1 is put in the column of the production function the corresponding row of which has been deleted. In the example in which only the intermediate products 1, 2 and 3 are alternatives matrix $EE$ is:

$$EE = \begin{bmatrix} 1 & 1 & 1 & 0 & 0 & \ldots & 0 \\ 0 & 0 & 0 & 1 & 0 & \ldots & 0 \\ 0 & 0 & 0 & 0 & 1 & \ldots & 0 \\ \cdot & \cdot & \cdot & \cdot & \cdot & & \cdot \\ \cdot & \cdot & \cdot & \cdot & \cdot & & \cdot \\ \cdot & \cdot & \cdot & \cdot & \cdot & & \cdot \\ 0 & 0 & 0 & 0 & 0 & \ldots & 0 \\ 0 & 0 & 0 & 0 & 0 & \ldots & 1 \end{bmatrix}$$

6.4. PLANNING, LINEAR PROGRAMMING AND UNIT COSTS

From the consideration of the procedures of standard cost accounting given in the previous sections it appears that these procedures are based on a number of assumptions. We shall mention the principal ones once again.

a. The quantities of the final products that must be produced are given.
b. If there is more than one production function per production centre, one has to indicate the production function relevant to the calculation of the unit costs. The basis for this indication is usually not discussed.

For giving a quantitative content to these assumptions we shall have to use planning procedures. Some of the best known techniques for solving a planning problem are those of linear programming (l.p.). The use of l.p. to give a quantitative content to the assumptions mentioned is obvious.

1. Quantifying the assumptions requires specification of a planning problem of relatively large extent. The techniques of l.p. can assist in finding a solution to these huge problems with the help of a computer.
2. The conditions for the solution of the planning problem with the help of l.p. are fulfilled. In particular, standard costing is based on homogeneously linear relations.
3. By describing the standard costing procedures, as we did in the previous sections, a specification of the planning problem can be chosen that links up directly with the one necessary for the accumulation of unit costs.

We shall try to prove the last point in this section.
   For the specification of the planning problem we distinguish three kinds of relations.

1. The *means of production relations* specify the relations between the production centres and the means of production. If the output has been defined in standard units of the intermediate or final product to be produced, then the production function can be written as a vector of technical coefficients. The collection of vectors can be represented by a matrix $A$, see (6.2). If, in addition, we start from the fact that there can be several production functions per production centre, the number of production functions will be larger than the total of the intermediate and final products. The matrix in which these possibilities are defined is $A$. Contrary to the procedure described in section 6.3, when using l.p. we do not start from a given vector $g$ of quantities to be produced, but from a vector $b_g$ with the available quantities of the means of production in a defined planning period. The vector $g$ now becomes an endogenous variable. The production factor relations are described as:

$$A_g \cdot g \leq b_g \qquad (6.22)$$

2. The *production specification relations* specify the relations between the

several production centres. These relations can be represented by, see (6.21)

$$(EE - {}_{,}C) \cdot g = \begin{bmatrix} 0 \\ 0 \\ \vdots \\ 0 \end{bmatrix} \qquad (6.23)$$

The equations indicate not only the characteristics of the relations between the production centres, but also the fact that the intermediate products are wholly distributed over the receiving production centres. This, in first instance, seems perhaps to restrict the possibility of describing the problem. However, it is not a relevant restriction. The equations (6.23) are balance equations defining the movements of goods. If one does not wish to accept a complete absorption one has to add variables specifying changes in inventories of the products concerned. This means adding two variables, namely the inventory of the relevant product at the beginning and at the end of the period.

3. The specification of the planning problem, as described by (6.22) and (6.23) can be solved with l.p. if we add a *value function* that must be optimized. In the specification given by us this means to be maximized. In the value function three groups of endogenous variables occur:

a. those of the production quantities of the final product
b. those of the production quantities of the intermediate product
c. those of the slack variables.

The so-called gross contribution margins can be chosen as the parameters of the production quantities of the final products in the value function. We define a *gross contribution margin* as the difference between the selling price and the direct variable costs per production function. The question arises what must be understood in this context by the direct variable costs. To answer the question, one can choose from several possibilities, which depend on the way in which $A_g$ is defined.

– If all means of production that are necessary for the production of product $j$ are incorporated in the production factor relations, the direct variable costs are equal to zero and in that situation the selling price and the gross contribution margin are the same. It is not probable that this situation will arise for the period for which we define the planning problem (see the next section).

- If the available quantities of some means of production in the planning period considered can be adapted to the desired quantities of the means of production, the relations between these means of production and the desired quantities of product $j$ can be left out of consideration. Then the product of technical coefficient and price ($a_{ij} \cdot p_i$) can be considered to be direct variable costs. These are deducted from the selling price in the value function of this of the production function concerned. In the case in which the production functions specify intermediate products the direct variable costs appear in the value function with a negative sign.
- One can imagine situations that can be considered to be combinations of the two just mentioned. Such situations occur, for example, when certain raw materials can be sold or when capacity can be reduced, for instance by leasing. Assuming that the available quantity of the means of production is given, we propose in that situation to incorporate the direct variable costs in the value function, but also to attach a parameter specifying the financial reward of the alternative output per unit to the slack variables concerned in the value function. The latter then looks as follows:

$$z = \sum_t -v_t \cdot g_t + \sum_s v_s \cdot g_s + \sum_l v_l \cdot x_l \qquad (6.24)$$

$v$ = the parameters in the value function; the indices $t$ and $s$ have the same content as in (6.11); the index $l$ specifies the number of slack variables

$g$ = the production quantities

$x$ = the slack variables.

In conclusion, the l.p. specification that could be used for the solution to the planning problem looks as follows:

$$\begin{aligned} &A_g \cdot g \leq b_g \\ &(EE - {}_rC) \cdot g = 0 \\ &\max! \ z = \sum_t -v_t \cdot g_t + \sum_s v_s \cdot g_s + \sum_l v_l \cdot x_l \end{aligned} \qquad (6.25)$$

In many cases a solution will result that violates the condition that all products incorporated in the assortment of the company should be produced. Then we have to add conditions to (6.25) specifying what could be called the *normal assortment* of the company. The l.p. specification then looks as follows:

$$\begin{aligned} &A_g \cdot g \leq b_g \\ &(EE - {}_rC) \cdot g = 0 \\ &EN \cdot g \geq n \\ &\max! \ z = \sum_t -v_t \cdot g_t + \sum_s v_s \cdot g_s + \sum_l v_l \cdot x_l \end{aligned} \qquad (6.26)$$

$n$ = a vector of the minimum quantities of all or certain final
products to be produced

$EN$ = a matrix representing the products defined in the normal
assortment. The structure of $EN$ is the same as of $EE$, because
it is possible that the constraints are fulfilled by using different
production functions per production centre.

The solution of (6.25) or (6.26) gives a quantitative content to the two
assumptions necessary for the standard costing procedure, which we have
mentioned at the beginning of this section. In fact, the optimum solution
consists of a vector $g_o$ of production quantities. This vector includes the
production quantities of all production centres, also those of the intermediate products. On the basis of $g_o$ the selected production function
or functions per production centre, i.e. the optimum way of production,
can be determined.

Given $g_o$, the unit costs can be calculated in a simple way, for which
the following operations must be carried out.

1. A reconstruction of matrix $A_g$ to matrix $A$. It is necessary
   a. to add to $A_g$ those means of production relations that were no
   potential restrictions;
   b. to combine the production functions chosen from $A_g$ in one production function per production centre. This can be achieved simply by
   defining a new comprehensive production function from the chosen
   ones with the help of a weighted arithmetical average using the
   relevant production quantities from $g_o$ as weights.
2. A vector $g$ must be derived from $g_o$ by adding the production quantities
   of the various selected production functions per production centre.
3. Given $A$ and $g$, $B$ can be calculated; see (6.2).
4. As $D$ in (6.11) is singular, we have to define a non-singular matrix $D^*$
   as:

$$D^* = (E - C) \cdot \hat{G}$$

5. The essence of the standard costing procedure can be represented as
   follows:

$$p' \cdot B = k_p' \cdot D^* \tag{6.27}$$

$p$ = a vector of prices
$k_p$ = a vector of unit costs

Eq. (6.27) says that the input defined in monetary units of the means of
production on the left-hand side must be equal to the internal deliveries
of the intermediate products and the external deliveries of the final pro-

ducts, both multiplied by their unit costs (in the Dutch literature the unit costs of the intermediate products are termed tariffs). The unknown in (6.27) is the vector $k_p$. It can be calculated if $D^*$ is non-singular.

$$k_p' = p' \cdot B \cdot (D^*)^{-1} \tag{6.28}$$

All calculations described in the previous sections can be carried out in the way described there, starting from (6.28).

The weakest point in the procedure seems to be the assumption that, given $B$, there is a known vector $p$, specified for the input of the means of production. In a number of cases, for instance for durable means of production, this assumption is not met; see section 6.2. If, however, $p_i$ is unknown, $k_i$, see (6.5), must be known. Then we must estimate $k_i$ apart from $b_i$. Since we are able to calculate $b_i$ in (6.26) without knowing $p_i$, we can calculate $p_i$ from:

$$p_i = \frac{k_i}{b_i} \tag{6.29}$$

For the calculation of $k_p$ one can therefore always start from $p_i$. If this applies, our procedure offers great advantages. For, the distinction between fixed and variable costs can be made on the basis of the fact whether (6.29) is used or not for defining $p_i$. If one wants to apply another method for calculating unit costs, for example the one of 'direct costing', then the whole calculation procedure can be maintained excepting the fact that the $p_i$ specified by (6.29) can be fixed at zero. As the differences in methods of calculating unit costs can practically all be reduced to a difference in defining fixed and variable costs on the one hand, and to a difference in specifying the elements of $p_i$ on the other, we believe that the calculation method described by us is applicable in all cases. If this statement is true, an important result has been reached, viz. that the discussions about the relevance of the various methods no longer focus on the alleged advantages of the calculation procedures, but only on *the* essential point – the choice of the assumptions.

## 6.5. PLANNING, BUDGETING AND COSTS

Starting from the historical development of costing and budgeting procedures, many differences and similarities between the two kinds of procedures might be indicated. We shall not do this here. Instead, we shall try to sketch a distinction and a correspondence between them, which are related to the functions they perform. In our opinion the correspondence can be found in a relation with the process of decision making in an organization. Prior to considering the process of decision making we make two restrictions.

1. Our exposition will be based on a normative description with the help of planning techniques.
2. We restrict our description of the collection of planning techniques to 1.p. To avoid misunderstanding, we emphatically point out that this restriction does not imply that we are of the opinion that 1.p. would be the most appropriate technique in all cases.

In the framework of the process of decision making with the help of planning techniques, we make a distinction as to the length of the planning period. In our opinion three periods can be distinguished.

1. The short period. This can vary from a day to a quarter of a year, which depends more or less on the character of the production process and the demand. We define budgeting as a collection of techniques directed towards the solution of the problems occurring in the short period.
2. The medium period. This runs from a quarter of a year to one or at most several years. The techniques of costing usually relate to this period.
3. The long period. This may vary from one year to a relatively large number of years. Generally, in organizations the length of the long period does not exceed ten years. The techniques used in this period are those usually termed strategic planning. However, the term strategic planning does not refer to a particular technique of planning or to particular characteristics of the process of planning.

We shall concentrate our analysis on two points:

a. our idea that from the point of view of deciding and planning a relationship should be established between the three periods of planning. However, we can only perfunctorily deal with this relationship;
b. the differences in the specification of the problem when applying 1.p. as a planning technique in each of the three cases. We shall consider these differences with regard to the following features:

– the degree of aggregation, especially the specification of matrix $A$
– the content of the parameters in the value function
– the assortment restriction
– the relation between the usual techniques of budgeting and planning and the techniques used by us.

We hope that through this discussion the differences and similarities between budgeting and costing will become obvious.

The most important function of budgeting is specifying a plan in which coordination of activities takes place. The characteristics of these activities are:

a. that they must be performed in the short period
b. that they are specified by a process of dealing with quite a number of data referring to the technical details.

The activities in the normal process of budgeting are generally not coordinated on a relatively detailed level. Coordination is carried out with the aid of a plan specifying the quantities to be produced and the inputs of the means of production. Using the symbols of the previous sections one could say that in budgeting a solution is sought for

$$A_b \cdot g_b = b_b \qquad\qquad (6.30)$$

where: $A_b$, $g_b$ and $b_b$ have the same content as the symbols we used; however, the specification of the coefficients differs for the situations we want to distinguish. If a solution is found for (6.30) (in practice this is usually realized by carrying out the calculation for several values of $g_b$ and $A_b$), the budgets per production centre can be specified. The *variable budgets* can be calculated for production centre $j$ from:

$$\sum_i a_{b(i,j)} \cdot p_i \qquad\qquad (6.31)$$

The *fixed budgets* for production centre $j$ are defined by $\sum k_j$ (see (6.29)). A solution to the problem in (6.30) can also be found by defining it as in (6.26). The advantage of the usage of (6.26) is that the calculation process is more efficient, since the arguments for finding a solution must in this case be quantified in the parameters of the value function. Using the features for describing the planning process we can distinguish the following characteristics of the planning problem in the short period:

a. The technical coefficients, as well as the description of the different methods of production, are based on the existing possibilities in the short period in the organization. As in the short period the set of constraints on the means of production will be great, of all specifications matrix $A_b$ will have the greatest number of means of production relations.

b. Since in $A_b$ most of the means of production relations occur, the direct variable costs to be taken into account can be low in number and in amount. However, this property may be superseded by the fact that one tries to find alternatives in the specification of $A_b$, for instance, by considering the possibility of casting off, boarding out, overwork, fine clauses for late delivery, etc. As we already noticed in section 6.4, such alternatives will often imply that the slack variables in the value function are given a parameter value unequal to zero. In many cases this means that other parameter values must also be applied to avoid inconsistent decisions.

c. The assortment restriction will in this case often play a central part. The assortment is hardly changeable in the short period. If the number of standing orders is large, often no solution can be found in the short period. In l.p. terms, there is no feasible solution. In this situation it is usually desirable to enlarge the number of alternatives, as has already been mentioned at b.

Besides the advantages mentioned of the use of l.p. for planning, it can be stated that with a formalization of the detail planning procedures a relationship between some of these procedures and l.p. can be found[8]. This relation divides the planning procedures in the short period in two groups. One group, see figure 6.1., deals with the detail decisions, the other with the global decisions. Budgeting as a planning vehicle coincides with the global decision procedures, budgeting as an instrument for control is related with the detail decisions. A relation between these groups of techniques offers two advantages:

a. Owing to the results of the detail production planning the consignment of budgets can be dispensed with. The detail production plan takes over the control function of the budget. It should be noticed that the l.p. specification can give the same information as the one in (6.30). Fixed and variable budgets are not instruments of planning, but its results. They are used to place the informal process of decision making about the details inside a certain framework. Formalizing this process makes the planning function of a budget superfluous.

b. Relationship between detail production plan procedures and l.p. budget plan procedures is desirable because then a link is made between the detail and global short period planning.

A relation is also desirable between the phases of planning in the short and in the medium period. From a planning point of view this relation could be established as follows.

1. The medium period includes a number of short periods which are mutually adjusted.

2. The specification in the medium period should leave open the possibility of linking it up with strategic planning.

To realize such possibilities, the specification in the medium period should possess the following characteristics.

a. It must be possible to subdivide the specification of $A$ into two or more short periods, which are related by interconnected balance equations. Through the extension of the specification a restriction will usually be made in the number of means of production relations. Besides, possibilities of considering new alternatives with regard both to the way of production and the assortment have to be incorporated into $A$. This may imply that technical coefficients are included in $A$ which do not describe the existing situation in the organization, but are related to a possible situation to be realized in this medium period or in one of the subsequent periods. We have already mentioned a possibility of getting information from the l.p. model about a situation to be realized. This concerns the difference between (6.25) and (6.26). If the result of the value function in (6.26) is considerably smaller than the one in (6.25), we can conclude that the assortment does not match the production apparatus or the reverse. With the help of l.p. one can investigate in what way a good adaptation can be specified and implemented.

b. The parameters in the value function shall have to be adapted to the alternatives. Moreover, one has to answer the question whether the slack variables in the value function have positive values and if so, what they are.

c. In the medium and long period the assortment specifications play a less central part than in the short period. In many cases the use of l.p. specifications will be indispensable for determining the relation between research and development programs and the existing production apparatus.

The purpose of the medium period planning is a coordination of decisions. To achieve this coordination one has to use aggregated variables. Aggregation must take place between global medium period planning and global short period planning on the one hand and between the activities of production centres on the other. As far as standard costing does use aggregate variables, it does contribute to the solution of the coordination problem. As we noticed in the previous section, the costing methods start from decisions that have already been taken with regard to a number of problems. Without taking these decisions also into consideration, the unit costs are a useless expedient for the coordination. If they are taken into consideration, as we proposed in section 6.4, the unit costs can be considered to be the basis for comparing several alternatives. This comparison relates especially to the consequences of the several alternatives in the long period. With this the unit costs become the expedient to connect medium and long period planning.

Besides the unit costs as a means to integrate medium and long period planning specifications one can claim that long period specifications must be built up from two or more medium periods. Given the volume of the specification existing in the medium period, generally the degree of aggregation of the variables will increase. There are, however, generally no fundamental differences between the specifications for a medium and a long period.

### 6.6. EXAMPLE

In this section we go into more detail in two aspects. The first is a schematic representation of the different phases of planning we distinguished. The second is a numerical example of the standard cost allocation procedure of section 6.4. In figure 6.1 we give a sketch of the various relations between the planning phases. The diagram is subdivided along two specifications. The first – in the vertical direction – has a subdivision in: input, decision processing, and output. The second – in horizontal direction – has a subdivision in: short period detail production planning, short period global production planning and medium period production planning. The symbols have the same meaning as in section 6.4 and 6.5. The relations between the different phases are specified.

The numerical example concerns point 1 of the output of the medium production planning period. We assume an organization producing three final products and five intermediate products. We distinguish six means of production. For four of the six we know a price per unit of the input, for the other two we only know the amount of costs in money per period. While dealing with the example we shall refer to the numbers of the equations we used in the previous sections. We start with a matrix $A$, see (6.2), (6.26) and (6.27).

$$A = \begin{bmatrix} 0.5 & 0.8 & 3.0 & 5.0 & 0.2 & 1.0 & 3.0 & 0 \\ 1.5 & 2.0 & 2.0 & 1.0 & 0.1 & 5.0 & 2.0 & 0 \\ 0 & 1.5 & 1.0 & 3.0 & 0 & 7.0 & 0.5 & 0 \\ 0.3 & 0.4 & 0 & 2.0 & 0 & 0 & 0 & 0 \\ 0.7 & 0 & 5.0 & 0 & 0.4 & 0 & 0 & 0 \\ 0 & 0.6 & 0.7 & 1.0 & 0.8 & 0 & 0 & 0 \end{bmatrix} \tag{6.32}$$

The first five production centres in (6.32) deliver the intermediate products. The last two rows of (6.32) are the means of production of which we do not know the price per unit of input. From the l.p. solution of the medium

EXAMPLE                                                                                              131

planning period we find a vector $g$, see (6.2) and (6.4), so we can calculate $B$.

$$g' = \begin{bmatrix} 5735375 & 4014062.5 & 816406.25 & 64500 & 23500 & 5000 & 2500 & 2000 \end{bmatrix} \tag{6.33}$$

Defining $g$ as a diagonal matrix one finds $B$ (see (6.2)), or, using equations (6.4), one finds:

$$b = \begin{bmatrix} 8867856.25 \\ 18380850.00 \\ 7067250.00 \\ 3455237.50 \\ 8106193.75 \\ 3063221.88 \end{bmatrix} \tag{6.34}$$

As we know $b_5$, $b_6$ and $k_5$, $k_6$, see (6.28), we can calculate $p_i$, $k_5 = 25,000$, $k_6 = 50,000$.

$$p_i = \begin{bmatrix} 10.- \\ 5.- \\ 3.- \\ 15.- \\ 0.03 \\ 0.16 \end{bmatrix} \tag{6.35}$$

In the next step we have to define $C$.

$$C = \begin{bmatrix} 0 & 1 & 2 & 1 & 0 & 4 & 0 & 2 \\ 0.25 & 0 & 3 & 0 & 5 & 1 & 3 & 0.5 \\ 0 & 0.1 & 0 & 5 & 3 & 2 & 4 & 1 \\ 0 & 0 & 0 & 0 & 2 & 1 & 5 & 0 \\ 0 & 0 & 0 & 0 & 0 & 3 & 1 & 3 \\ 0 & 0 & 0 & 0 & 0 & 0 & 0 & 0 \\ 0 & 0 & 0 & 0 & 0 & 0 & 0 & 0 \\ 0 & 0 & 0 & 0 & 0 & 0 & 0 & 0 \end{bmatrix} \tag{6.36}$$

In the final step we have to calculate $D^*$, see (6.27).

$$D^* = \begin{bmatrix} 5735375.00 & -4014062.50 & -1632812.50 & -64500 & 0 & -200 \\ -1433843.75 & 4014062.50 & -2449218.75 & 0 & -117500 & -50 \\ 0 & -401406.25 & 816406.25 & -322500 & -70500 & -100 \\ 0 & 0 & 0 & 64500 & -47500 & -50 \\ 0 & 0 & 0 & 0 & 28500 & -150 \\ 0 & 0 & 0 & 0 & 0 & 50 \\ 0 & 0 & 0 & 0 & 0 & \\ 0 & 0 & 0 & 0 & 0 & \end{bmatrix}$$

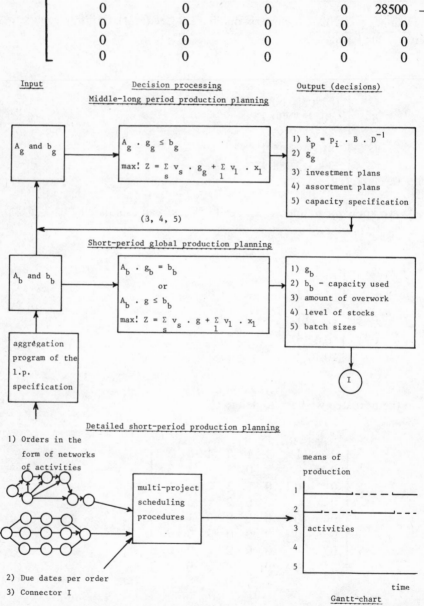

Fig. 6.1

EXAMPLE                                                                    133

$$\left.\begin{array}{rr} 0 & -4000 \\ -7500 & -1000 \\ 10000 & -2000 \\ 12500 & 0 \\ -2500 & -6000 \\ 0 & 0 \\ 2500 & 0 \\ 0 & 2000 \end{array}\right] \quad (6.37)$$

All the data necessary to calculate the vector of cost prices, see (6.28), are now specified.

$$k_p = \begin{bmatrix} 50.37 \\ 133.38 \\ 544.13 \\ 2865.18 \\ 8032.28 \\ 28441.11 \\ 24976.33 \\ 24808.38 \end{bmatrix} \quad (6.38)$$

Concluding this article we would like to make two final remarks.

1. In the matrix $A$ in (6.32) we defined a production centre for a final product without means of production relations. As we have discovered, this is a situation that often occurs in practice. It happens in all such situations where there is no group of means of production used only for the production of one of the final products. In that case the production centre of the final product becomes artificial. It is used to gather all the deliveries. The sense of such a gathering is to create the possibility of comparing the different products as far as their costs of production are concerned.
2. In our example we assumed that we knew the vector $g$ through l.p. If one does not use l.p., it is often difficult to calculate the production quantities of the production centres delivering intermediate products. If there are no return deliveries between production centres, one can use the so-called Gozinto graph procedure to calculate the sub-vector $g_t$. For that purpose one can use the formula:

$$(E - C)^{-1} \cdot g_{s-t} = g \quad (6.39)$$

If there are return deliveries, as in our example, the formula is not usable without a number of changes. The whole problem can, however, directly be solved by using l.p.

NOTES

1. J. Johnston, *Statistical Cost Analysis*, New York, 1960. G. J. Benston, 'Multiple regression analysis of cost behavior', *Accounting Review*, October 1966.
2. P. F. Ostwald, *Cost Estimating for Engineering and Management*, Englewood Cliffs, N.J., 1974.
3. A. L. Thomas, *The Allocation Problem in Financial Accounting Theory*, American Accounting Association, 1969.
4. If one wants to take into account products that are intermediate as well as final, then one will have to define an element in both subvectors, e.g. $g_3$ and $g_{t+3}$. In this case the technical coefficient $c_{3, t+3} = 1$ and the technical coefficient $c_{t+3, 3} = 0$.
5. Other technical coefficients can also be equal to zero.
6. In practice one simplifies the procedure of the allocation of indirect costs by approximating the matrix $F$ by a triangular matrix $_t F$ (being a submatrix of $F$, containing the first $t$ rows and $t$ columns of $F$). If the elements under the main diagonal of $_t F$ equal zero, then the equations (6.14a) and (6.14b) can be solved successively as follows:

$$W_1 = U_1$$

$$\vdots$$

$$W_h = U_h + \sum_{x=1}^{h-1} f_{xh} \cdot W_x \quad (h = 2, 3, 4, \ldots, t)$$

In the literature this procedure is known as the 'allocation from left to right'. When using this procedure, it is not possible to take into account the return deliveries $d_{xh}, x > h$.
7. The technique of cost allocation shows correspondence with the techniques of input-output analysis. See among others: F. Vogel, *Betriebliche Strukturbilanzen und Struktur-Analysen*, Würzburg, 1969; H. Münstermann, *Unternehmungsrechnung*, Wiesbaden, 1969.
8. See for a general description of the interrelations between short period global planning where a matrix specification is used, and short period detail planning, J. H. Mize, C. R. White and G. H. Brooks, *Operations Planning and Control*, Englewood Cliffs, N.J., 1971; for an explanation of the relation between short period global planning with the help of l.p. and short period detail planning, A. Bosman, 'Lineaire programmering, kosten- en kostprijsberekening', *Maandblad voor Accountancy en Bedrijfshuishoudkunde* 47 (1973), nrs. 5/6.

# 7. Stochastic budgeting *

T. KLOEK and H. A. VAN DER DONK

## 7.1. INTRODUCTION

The budget of a firm attempts to reflect:

- the expectations regarding developments outside and inside the firm;
- the strategy envisaged in view of the objective of the firm.

The budget usually consists of a numerical presentation and an explanation of the main view-points underlying the numerical presentation. In this way, the intention of the budget is only partially realized. For such a presentation only reflects one possible development of the firm. This development is conditional. It is entirely dependent on the accuracy of the underlying assumptions.

However, in most cases differences occur between these assumptions and reality, so that the budget fails to materialize. This has two causes:

- Internal factors (such as the use of factors of production) are imperfectly controlled.
- External factors are imperfectly forecasted. This is true of reactions by others to our own strategy (e.g., reactions of demand to selling prices), as well as of other external factors (e.g., general business conditions).

In this article, we describe a method which does take account of these uncertainties. Use is made of the concept of probability and of a few concepts and techniques of probability theory. We intend to clarify these concepts also for the statistically untrained reader by giving as many examples and using as few technical terms as possible.

The method to be discussed has been developed at the Netherlands Railways and is called 'interval budgeting method'. Briefly, it amounts to the following. The budget is computed several times based on different assumptions. Most weight is attached to the most likely assumptions. Using a computer and some results from statistical theory, the number of

* This article is a translation of 'Het taxeren van onzekerheid bij het opstellen van een begroting', published in *Maandblad voor Accountancy en Bedrijfshuishoudkunde* 50(1976), pp. 149–160.

cases considered can easily be made very large. This gives the opportunity of assessing the existing uncertainties. The term 'assessing' is used because the method has in common with the well-known instances of assessing the feature that an honest judgement is supposed to be given to the best of one's knowledge, even though a certain degree of subjectivity cannot be avoided. This subjectivity need be no great drawback since the assessments of various experts will usually not differ very much and one can, in the end, always take an average. Besides, the phenomenon of subjectivity appears everywhere where assessments have to be made. In business, all sorts of assessors are accepted. There is no reason why a different view of the assessment of uncertainty should be taken. The description of the interval budgeting method will be illustrated by examples taken from the Netherlands Railways. The method can be applied to any firm or organization, provided a computer is available.

In sections 7.2, 7.3, and 7.4, some concepts of probability theory are introduced and examples are given. In section 7.5, the computer program for the interval budgeting method is discussed. Section 7.6 is devoted to the choice of the interval boundaries relevant to the policy of the firm, and section 7.7 contains concluding remarks. The appendices present a flow chart of the computer program INTPRO, a fictitious Netherlands Railways budget for 1971, and a short discussion of a formal definition of the concept of subjective probability.

## 7.2. PROBABILITY DISTRIBUTIONS

The concept of subjective probability coincides so closely with common usage that we can use the notion without giving a formal definition. This approach is followed in this section. A short discussion of a formal definition is given in appendix 7.3.

In making an interval budget, we proceed as follows. For every relevant variable (e.g., real national income growth or wage-rate development), we estimate between what values it may vary and what probabilities should be attributed to these intervals. A prerequisite for the application is, of course, that one can conceive the intervals and the associated probabilities. Experiences from the past and analytical insight will, as a rule, enable one to do this. In this connection, it should be realized that an intelligent guess is to be preferred to a quasi-definite statement in which existing uncertainty is ignored. An example may clarify this.

In every Netherlands Railways budget, wage-rate development plays an important part, both directly in the item of personnel cost and indirectly in items like transport by third parties and maintenance by third parties. In the usual comments to the budget it may, for instance, be stated: 'an

*Table 7.1.*   Probability distribution of possible wage-rate increases (fictitious numbers).

| wage-rate increases (percentages) | estimated probability (percentages) |
|---|---|
| less than 6 | 0 |
| 6 or more, less than  7 | 5 |
| 7 or more, less than  8 | 15 |
| 8 or more, less than  9 | 30 |
| 9 or more, less than 10 | 20 |
| 10 or more, less than 11 | 10 |
| 11 or more, less than 12 | 7 |
| 12 or more, less than 13 | 5 |
| 13 or more, less than 14 | 4 |
| 14 or more, less than 15 | 2 |
| 15 or more, less than 16 | 2 |
| 16 or more | 0 |
|  | 100 |

increase in wages of $8\frac{1}{2}\%$ has been assumed'. In the interval budgeting method this statement is replaced by a number of statements as given in table 7.1.

The differences from the traditional approach are evident. The probability of wage increases other than $8\frac{1}{4}\%$ (or between 8 and 9%) is stressed. The various possibilities (as defined by the intervals) are matched by pre-supposed probabilities. Thus, the reader may make sure whether a larger wage increase is deemed more or less probable than a smaller by the maker of the budget.

A presentation as given in table 7.1 is called probability distribution, or just distribution. Probabilities must satisfy two formal constraints. They must be non-negative and, after all possibilities have been exhaustively listed, they must add up to one (or 100%).

Let us return to the example. This item of personnel cost is determined by yet another important element, viz., the number of employees. It cannot be stated exactly in advance how this number will develop, even though one sees the tendency of a yearly decrease. Hence, we have again uncertainty and again the possibility of formalizing uncertainty in a distribution, as given in table 7.2.

Note that the distribution is symmetrical. Starting from the centre (1000), we find the same probabilities in both directions (30, 15, and 5%). This is contrary to table 7.1 in which we deal with an asymmetrical or skew distribution.

The distribution of table 7.2 must be combined with one regarding the wage-rate development in order to derive a distribution of personnel cost. We come back to this in section 7.5.

*Table 7.2.*  Probability distribution of possible decreases in personnel numbers (fictitious numbers).

| decrease in personnel (numbers) | estimated probability (percentages) |
|---|---|
| less than 800 | 5 |
| between 800 and 899 | 15 |
| between 900 and 999 | 30 |
| between 1000 and 1099 | 30 |
| between 1100 and 1199 | 15 |
| 1200 and over | 5 |
| | 100 |

The balance of all budget items is the loss or profit. If one or more budget items figure as a distribution rather than as a unique amount, then also profit or loss can only be represented by a distribution.

### 7.3. SOME SPECIFIC DISTRIBUTIONS

The tables presented in section 7.2 indicate the probabilities that the variable concerned will assume a value within a number of intervals. Often a slightly different presentation is used in which the intervals are added from low to high (The reverse is also possible but less common). In this way, table 7.3 is derived from table 7.1. This cumulative probability distribution is called distribution function. We come back to this tabulated form of representing a distribution in section 7.5.

*Table 7.3.*  Distribution function of possible wage-rate increases.

| wage-rate increases (percentages) less than: | estimated probability (percentages) |
|---|---|
| 6 | 0 |
| 7 | 5 |
| 8 | 20 |
| 9 | 50 |
| 10 | 70 |
| 11 | 80 |
| 12 | 87 |
| 13 | 92 |
| 14 | 96 |
| 15 | 98 |
| 16 | 100 |

In many instances one can make use of symmetrical distributions of the type derived from the normal or Gauss curve. This has a great advantage with respect to the data processing. Such a distribution is characterized by the mean ($\mu$) and the standard deviation ($\sigma$). The latter is a measure of the dispersion, i.e., the 'width' of the distribution. In the case of a normal distribution, the probability of a value between $\mu - \sigma$ and $\mu + \sigma$ is 0.68, the probability of a value between $\mu - 2\sigma$ and $\mu + 2\sigma$ is 0.95, and the probability of a value between $\mu - 3\sigma$ and $\mu + 3\sigma$ is 0.9973 or about $99\frac{3}{4}\%$. This leads to a third possibility of formulating probabilities, as follows. Energy consumption, for instance, lies with a probability of

68% between 56 and 60 million guilders
95% between 54 and 62 million guilders
$99\frac{3}{4}\%$ between 52 and 64 million guilders.

## 7.4. RELATIONS BETWEEN THE VARIABLES

Every production process shows relations between, on the one hand, production volume and, on the other, input quantities used (in other words, one variable depends on another). Relations also exist between the prices and the quantities of input. These relations can either be automatic or follow from the policy pursued by the firm. An example of an automatic relation in Netherlands Railways is the increase in energy input when the transport of goods increases. An example of a relation that follows from the firm's policy is the accelerated introduction of labour-saving techniques if wages rise faster than was anticipated. Furthermore, we should distinguish between relations effective within one budget period only and relations effective in the longer run. The example of the energy input belongs to the first category, the example of the labour-saving techniques to the second, especially if investments are needed to achieve the effect.

In the examples, the relations prevailing as a consequence of dependences partly compensate each other in financial terms. But this is not always the case. For instance, a very bad winter abundant in ice and snow will bring about high costs for heating (carriages, buildings, switch-points), traction energy, and maintenance of rolling-stock. At the same time, under such circumstances, the love of travel of the public is in total often less than normal. As a consequence, extra costs are not compensated (not even partially) by higher receipts. However, compensating dependences occur more often than reinforcing dependences.

In the management process one should certainly try to take account of the existing relations. However, this is possible to a limited extent only in the example of the railways, since the production process of such a firm is subject – in the short run – to many rigidities. A clear example of this phenomenon is given by the time-table of passenger transport. This time-table is fixed for six or twelve months. A larger or smaller volume of transport has hardly any immediate influence on cost. But the volume of transport can have effects in the longer run (viz., in subsequent time-tables). The interrelations between budget items will, therefore, primarily show up in budgets extending over several years.

Assume, for instance, that a (possible) wage explosion in year I will induce the management of a firm to reduce personnel numbers in year I + 1 more strongly than in the case of a more normal wage increase. The distribution of the labour force in year I + 1 will then be dependent on the possible wage-rate increase in year I. The situation can be handled by attributing a variable average to the decrease in personnel numbers. This can be very simply realized in the context of a computer program, as will turn out in the next section.

Apart from the interrelations in real terms mentioned above, inter-relations exist in financial terms that do have effect in the short run. In this connection, one can think of the effects of wage-rate increases that influence items like maintenance, materials, etc., apart from the personnel item. The degree to which these items are influenced of course depends on the share of wages in the items concerned.

### 7.5. COMPUTER PROGRAM

The problems described in the preceding sections with respect to:

– various probability distributions,
– combinations of distributions (e.g., personnel cost = average wage rate × personnel numbers, where average wage rate and personnel numbers each have their own probability distribution),
– interrelations between variables,

make the use of a computer unavoidable since no simple formulae exist by which all problems can be solved simultaneously.

The simulation approach is the obvious choice. In this approach, a large number of drawings (say, 10,000) are made from each relevant distribution.

The computer program developed for this purpose is called INTPRO (= INTerval PROgnosis). It is based on three kinds of distribution:

1. Normal distributions. These are determined by two parameters: the mean, $\mu$, and the standard deviation, $\sigma$.

2. $t$-Distributions. These occur when econometric relations are used to estimate certain budget items. In Netherlands Railways this is the case with the demand function for passenger transport. The parameters to be used are $\mu$, $\sigma$, and the number of degrees of freedom.
3. Other distributions. Any arbitrary distribution can be approximated by a tabulated distribution function like the one for wage-rate increases of table 7.3.

By means of built-in transformations, dependences between various budget items are taken account of. For instance:

$$\text{WSUM(I)} = \text{PERS(I}-1)*(1+\text{RPERS(I)})*\text{WAGE(I}-1)*$$
$$(1+\text{RWAGE(I)})$$

where

| | |
|---|---|
| WSUM | = wage sum |
| PERS | = personnel numbers |
| RPERS | = relative change in personnel numbers (as a fraction) |
| WAGE | = average wage rate per head |
| RWAGE | = relative change in average wage rate per head (as a fraction) |
| I | = year of prognosis |
| I − 1 | = preceding year. |

The relation above is nothing but a reformulation of the definition equation:

$$\text{WSUM(I)} = \text{PERS(I)}*\text{WAGE(I)}$$

The reformulation enables us to combine the known data PERS(I − 1) and WAGE(I − 1) with probability distributions for the relative changes RPERS and RWAGE.

Another simple example is the following:

$$\text{MAMAT(I)} = \text{MAMAT(I}-1)*(1+0.7*\text{RWAGE(I)}+0.3*$$
$$\text{RPRICE(I)})$$

where

| | |
|---|---|
| MAMAT | = expenditures on maintenance and materials |
| RPRICE | = relative change of the price level (as a fraction). |

In this case, drawings from the probability distributions for RWAGE and RPRICE are combined with the known item MAMAT(I − 1) and the wage and materials shares in MAMAT. If one expects substitution effects to occur owing to the wage-rate and price-level increases, one can also replace the constants 0.7 and 0.3 by variables. One can even add a stochastic variable as a component.

Our third example concerns the relation between a wage-rate increase in a given year and a decrease in the labour force one year later. We mentioned this relation in the preceding section. In a computer program for a budget extending over several years this relation could be represented as follows:

$$RPERS(I + 1) = RPERSN(I + 1) - 0.5*(RWAGE(I) - 0.085)$$

where

RPERSN = the normal relative change in personnel numbers (as a fraction).

This means that for every per cent wage-rate increase in year I in excess of the $8\frac{1}{2}\%$ that is considered normal the labour force in year I+1 will be reduced one half per cent more than is considered normal. If one finds this relation too exact, one may add a random deviation.

As an illustration, appendix 7.1 presents a flow chart of the program INTPRO and appendix 7.2 a table of a fictitious budget for 1971. It is seen from appendix 7.2 that the intervals belonging to the (sub-)totals are smaller than those obtained by subtracting the sum of the corresponding lower boundaries from the sum of the corresponding upper boundaries. This is a normal rule implying, again, that it is difficult to make interval budgets without the aid of a computer. For an explanation of this rule some technical concepts from probability theory are needed.[1]

### 7.6. INTERVAL BOUNDARIES AND POLICY

Employment of the concept of probability by management at various hierarchical levels facilitates the designation of boundaries at which action should be taken. The experience with the notion of probability conceived as a relative frequency (e.g., in the area of quality control) is to a large extent applicable here. Consider the case of a normally distributed variable. Often, an interval with a probability of 95 % (i.e., between $\mu - 2\sigma$ and $\mu + 2\sigma$) is chosen. We have seen that if boundaries of three times the standard deviation are chosen, only in $\frac{1}{4}$ % of all cases (hence, practically never) one of the boundaries is exceeded. The possibility of intervention is then virtually nil because the responsible person can always claim to be within acceptable boundaries. If, on the other hand, boundaries of one standard deviation are chosen, there is a 32 % (100–68) probability that one of the boundaries is exceeded by pure chance. This leads to frequent interventions which will mostly be unjustifiable. As a consequence, attention of management is distracted from more important questions and the atmosphere in the firm is disturbed.

It depends on the nature of the individual budget item how big a tolerance interval should be chosen in each particular case. A few factors playing some part here are:

- the amount of money involved
- the possible influence on the firm's net results
- the possible influence on the availability of investment funds
- the possibility of taking corrective or compensating measures and the rate of realization needed for them to have effect.

### 7.7. CONCLUDING REMARKS

1. The techniques described in this article are intended to assess as accurately as possible the magnitude of the existing margins of uncertainty. They are not intended (and not suitable) to reduce these margins.
2. In estimating probability functions of the type described, one is liable to make two kinds of mistakes. Suppose the true estimate of an interval with a probability of 95 % is between 90 and 110. One may then underestimate the existing uncertainty by choosing, for instance, the interval between 98 and 102. If this is done systematically, frequent, perhaps unpleasant, surprises may occur afterwards. One may also overestimate the existing uncertainty by choosing, for instance, the interval between 50 and 150. In this case, one is always right but valuable information is withheld from management. Evidently, both kinds of mistakes should be avoided as best as one can.
3. It is recommended that a budget compiled using the procedure described here should be frequently updated, for instance, every two or three months, in order to permit of a flexible policy. By incorporating newly available information into the budget the margins of uncertainty can often be reduced.

### NOTES

1. In the case of normally distributed variables, the intervals are proportional to the standard deviations. We have:

$$\sigma_1 + \sigma_2 \geqq \sqrt{\sigma_1^2 + \sigma_2^2 + 2\rho\,\sigma_1\,\sigma_2}$$

(where $\rho$ = the correlation coefficient), as can be easily verified by squaring. The equality sign holds only in the extreme case when $\rho = 1$. This rule is true under more general conditions but the theorem cannot be proved in this article.

# APPENDIX 7.1. Flow-chart of computer program

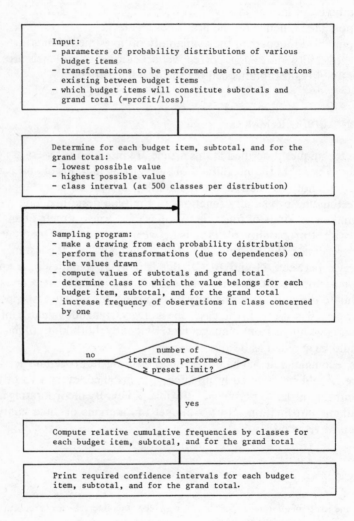

Input:
- parameters of probability distributions of various budget items
- transformations to be performed due to interrelations existing between budget items
- which budget items will constitute subtotals and grand total (=profit/loss)

Determine for each budget item, subtotal, and for the grand total:
- lowest possible value
- highest possible value
- class interval (at 500 classes per distribution)

Sampling program:
- make a drawing from each probability distribution
- perform the transformations (due to dependences) on the values drawn
- compute values of subtotals and grand total
- determine class to which the value belongs for each budget item, subtotal, and for the grand total
- increase frequency of observations in class concerned by one

number of iterations performed ≥ preset limit?

no

yes

Compute relative cumulative frequencies by classes for each budget item, subtotal, and for the grand total

Print required confidence intervals for each budget item, subtotal, and for the grand total.

# APPENDIX 7.2.  Interval exploitation budget*

| Receipts | Interval** | Point estimate |
|---|---|---|
| 1. Passenger transport | 421.1 – 437.7 | 429.7 |
| 2. Goods transport | 341.4 – 367.8 | 356.6 |
| 3. Other transport | 40.7 – 44.3 | 42.5 |
| Subtotal 1 – 3 | 810.7 – 842.9 | 828.8 |
| 4. Other receipts | 27.2 – 28.2 | 27.7 |
| 5. Dividends from participations | 2.1 – 3.1 | 2.6 |
| Subtotal 4 – 5 | 29.6 – 31.0 | 30.3 |
| Subtotal 1 – 5 | 841.1 – 873.1 | 859.1 |
| 6. Government contribution | – | 105.0 |
| Subtotal 1 – 6 | 946.1 – 978.1 | 964.1 |
| | | |
| *Costs* | | |
| 7. Personnel | 647.5 – 694.1 | 663.1 |
| 8. Maintenance | – | 185.2 |
| 9. Energy | 88.0 – 91.1 | 88.9 |
| 10. Delegated transport | 115.6 – 120.4 | 118.0 |
| 11. Sundries | – | 30.4 |
| Subtotal 7 – 11 | 1070.4 – 1117.3 | 1085.6 |
| 12. To capital account | – | – 104.0 |
| Subtotal 7 – 12 | 966.4 – 1013.3 | 981.6 |
| (=net exploitation costs) | | |
| 13. Retained payments | – | 4.0 |
| 14. Other costs | – | 3.0 |
| 15. Depreciation allowances | 141.6 – 143.8 | 141.9 |
| 16. Interest | 51.7 – 54.9 | 52.6 |
| Subtotal 7 – 16 | 1167.7 – 1217.3 | 1183.1 |
| Grand total 1 – 16 | 201.4 – 256.0 | 219.0 |
| (Loss balance) | | |

*Netherlands Railways, 1971 (in millions of guilders, fictitious numbers).
**Interval = range within which the results will be with 95% probability.

# APPENDIX 7.3.    A definition of subjective probability

The simplest formal definition of the concept of subjective probability is given by Pratt, Raiffa and Schlaifer[1]. They employ a so-called canonical experiment. Using a canonical experiment, one can generate stochastic variables with arbitrarily chosen objective probabilities. Such an experiment may comprise drawing a number from a bag with a hundred numbers or turning a (tested) roulette wheel. If, for instance, the numbers are from 1 to 100, then the probability of drawing a number less than or equal to 37 is equal to 0.37.

Suppose you may choose between the following alternatives:

1. you receive a prize A (whether this be a bottle of cognac or a tour around the world is immaterial) if wages (to be defined exactly, e.g., average yearly wage rate at Netherlands Railways) rise less than 12% next year;
2. you receive the same prize A as sub (1) and at the same moment, if a number is drawn less than or equal to 80.

Now if you are indifferent to (1) or (2), you assess at 80% (implicitly) the probability that wages rise less than 12% next year. If you prefer (1) to (2), you assess this probability at over 80%; if, however, you prefer (2) to (1), then you assess this probability at less than 80%. In the latter two cases one can, by changing alternative (2), try to determine at what percentage you do assess this probability.

The probability concept described here is more closely related to common usage than is the traditional probability concept of relative frequency. The formal theory has been developed by De Finetti and Savage. A simple and clear introduction is given by: H. Raiffa, *Decision Analysis*, Addison Wesley, 1968.

NOTES

1. J. W. Pratt, H. Raiffa and R. Schlaifer, ' The foundations of decision under uncertainty: an elementary exposition', *Journal of the American Statistical Association* 59 (1965), 353 – 75.

# 8.  Variance analysis, flexible budgeting and responsibility accounting

C. B. TILANUS and J. A. M. THEEUWES

A *variance* in accounting is the difference between two amounts one of which is the basic, standard, or reference amount and the other the comparable amount. *Variance analysis* is concerned with breaking down the difference between the two amounts into meaningful parts.

*Flexible budgeting*, as opposed to fixed budgeting, specifies different expense or cost allowances for different levels of activity. Thus, budgeted cost rates are viewed as functions rather than constants fixed beforehand.

*Responsibility accounting* tries to impute costs (and proceeds) to the persons responsible for them in order that the accounting figures may serve as feedback signals for better management. Responsibility accounting has a direct bearing on the breakdown of variances into meaningful parts.

It is proposed to show in this article the links between the three concepts. The cost functions to be employed will be quite general, including proportionally variable costs and fixed costs as extreme cases. The analysis is based on causal relationships. A causal relationship between two variables exists if the first variable is a function of the second; i.e., the first depends on the second, or the first is the effect and the second is the cause. Special attention is paid to the problem of different time periods in budgeting. For example, long term and short term are distinguished.

In section 8.1, some classical solutions to the problem of variance analysis are stated. In section 8.2, the flexible-budgeting approach to variance analysis is introduced. It is shown in section 8.3 that the approach can easily by applied to multi-stage, multidimensional situations. Appendices 8.1 and 8.2 contain the algebra of the two-stage, two-dimensional and three-dimensional cases, respectively, and a numerical example of the latter.

## 8.1. CLASSICAL VARIANCE ANALYSIS

Variance analysis is usually dealt with in a mathematically simple way and has been a subject of discussion for a long time. Our earliest reference is an article by Amerman in 1953 [1]. The subject has been mathematically treated a number of times, see, amongst others, [1, 5, 6, 10, 11, 12]. The reason that the 'simple mathematics of variance analysis' is discussed time and again is that different authors prefer different solutions and that different special cases are selected for exemplification [2, 3, 4, 7]. In this section, the problem will be stated in classical terms.

Consider the difference between a basic and a comparable amount. In this section, we shall use the terms budgeted $(B)$ for the basic and actual $(A)$ for the comparable amount. If the amounts are themselves one-dimensional, then so is the difference and no meaningful breakdown is possible. Examples of one-dimensional amounts are cash in hand or items in stock.

Cost items $(C)$ are often two- or three-dimensional. In the two-dimensional case, the two variates may in general be called quantity produced $(Q)$ and cost rate $(R)$. For instance, total labour cost of the output produced is the volume of output multiplied by the labour cost rate per unit of output.

The two-dimensional case is illustrated by figure 8.1. Budgeted costs are given by the area $C_B = Q_B \times R_B$, actual cost by the area $C_A = Q_A \times R_A$. An obvious breakdown of the total variance $C_A - C_B$ is into three partial variances:

– the area $(Q_A - Q_B) \times R_B$, which may be called quantity variance
– the area $Q_B \times (R_A - R_B)$, which may be called rate variance
– the area $(Q_A - Q_B) \times (R_A - R_B)$, which may be called joint variance.

Note that both the difference $Q_A - Q_B$ and the difference $R_A - R_B$ may be either positive, zero, or negative. Graphically, illustration of all cases would call for $3 \times 3 = 9$ figures. Mathematically, however, the analysis is the same in each case. For clarity of presentation we content ourselves with figure 8.1 in which both differences are positive.

Whereas the quantity variance is allocated to $Q$ and the rate variance to $R$, there are two possibilities for the allocation of the joint variance of $Q$ and $R$, viz., either to $Q$ or to $R$. Alternatively, one may take the agnostic view that it is impossible to allocate the joint variance, or one may further break down the joint variance into a part allocated to $Q$ and a part allocated to $R$, the division being either in half, or in the ratio of the areas $[(Q_A - Q_B) \times R_B]$: $[Q_B \times (R_A - R_B)]$, or in the ratio of the relative lengths $[(Q_A - Q_B)/Q_B]$: $[(R_A - R_B)/R_B]$.

In the three-dimensional case, we may in general call the three variates quantity produced $(Q)$, factor usage per unit of output $(F)$, and price per unit of the production factor $(P)$. For instance, raw material costs of output are quantity produced, multiplied by raw material usage per unit of output and by price per unit of raw material.

An elementary breakdown of the total variance in the three-dimensional case would give rise to three single variances (of quantity, factor usage, and price), three joint variances of two variates ($Q$ and $F$, $Q$ and $P$, and $F$ and $P$) and one joint variance of all three variates. The number of possible alloca-

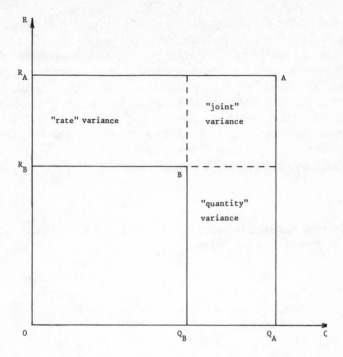

*Fig. 8.1.* Classical, two-dimensional variance analysis.

tions of the joint variances increases factorially. For instance, one may allocate the joint variances in $2 \times 2 \times 2 \times 3 = 24$ ways to any one of the variates without any further breakdown.

The problem, however, is not to extend the number of possible mathematical solutions for the breakdown of total variance but rather to find a meaningful breakdown as a tool for management. Therefore, variance analysis is treated as part of budgeting control. Use is to be made of the concepts of flexible budgeting and responsibility accounting.

## 8.2. THE FLEXIBLE-BUDGETING APPROACH TO VARIANCE ANALYSIS

Consider a decentralized organization in which flexible budgeting and responsibility accounting is applied. How does this affect variance analysis? Different persons will be responsible for different variables in the organization. For instance, take a two-dimensional cost item $(C)$, the product of quantity produced $(Q)$ and cost rate $(R)$. One man, perhaps from a commercial department, will be responsible for $Q$ and another, perhaps from a production department, will be responsible for $R$. Hence, just as in classical variance analysis, partial variances have to be allocated to variates in order that responsibility accounting may be effective.

Now flexible budgeting provides the key for the breakdown of total variance between actual and budgeted cost. For $R$ is a function of $Q$; $Q$ is cause and $R$ is effect. Hence, if actual $Q$ deviates from budgeted $Q$, this entails a functional deviation of $R$ caused by the deviation of $Q$. The functional deviation should be attributed to $Q$. Besides, actual $R$ may show a genuine deviation from what $R$ would have been, had $Q$ been budgeted as $Q_A$. The latter deviation should be attributed to $R$.

Algebraically, let budgeted $R$ be a function of $Q$:

$$R_B = R_B(Q)$$

Then the total variance between actual cost $(C_A)$ and budgeted cost $(C_B)$ should be broken down as follows:

$$
\begin{aligned}
C_A - C_B &= Q_A \times R_A - Q_B \times R_B(Q_B) \\
&= Q_A \times [R_A - R_B(Q_A)] \\
&+ Q_A \times [R_B(Q_A) - R_B(Q_B)] \\
&+ [Q_A - Q_B] \times R_B(Q_B)
\end{aligned}
$$

partial variance attributable to:

| |
|---|
| $R$ |
| $Q$ (indirect) |
| $Q$ (direct) |

In figure 8.2, the above variances are shown for the case where all differences are positive. The reader is requested to consider the areas corresponding to partial variances with flexible budgeting as given in figure 8.2 and to compare them to the areas corresponding to partial variances in classical variance analysis as shown in figure 8.1.

Note that the budgeting curve for $R$ in figure 8.2 has deliberately been so drawn as to indicate a completely arbitrary curve. If the relationship between $R$ and $Q$ is defined in functional form, then this function is completely arbitrary. Alternatively, the relationship between $R$ and $Q$ may be given in tabular form (see appendix 8.2 for an example). Again, the values in the table showing $R$ for given $Q$ are completely arbitrary. As a consequence, all of the above differences may be positive, zero, or negative. Mathematically, this makes no difference to the breakdown. Figure 8.2 gives an illustration of the case where all differences are positive.

Note also that in this analysis nothing is said about the nature of costs, whether they are variable, semi-variable, or fixed. If one defines semi-variable costs as anything between the extreme cases of proportionally variable and fixed costs, one might say that the case of semi-variable costs is considered. However, the extreme cases are also covered by the analysis. Mathematically, it makes no difference to the breakdown whether we are concerned with variable or fixed costs or something in between. Graphic-

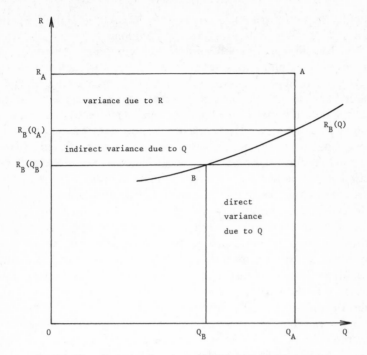

*Fig. 8.2.* Two-dimensional variance analysis with flexible budgeting.

ally, in the case of variable, i.e. strictly proportional, costs the curve of $R$ as a function of $Q$ would reduce to a horizontal straight line; in the case of fixed costs the curve would reduce to a hyperbola. One can easily verify that in the case of proportionally variable costs ($R_B(Q_A) = R_B(Q_B) =$ constant) the indirect partial variance of $Q$ would vanish; whereas in the case of fixed costs ($R_B(Q_A) = C_B/Q_A, R_B(Q_B) = C_B/Q_B$) the total variance to be attributed to $Q$ (direct plus indirect) would vanish.

## 8.3. MULTI-STAGE, MULTIDIMENSIONAL VARIANCE ANALYSIS

The flexible-budgeting approach to variance analysis can straightforwardly be extended to more than one stage and more than two dimensions.

By variance analysis in stages or steps we mean the following. The total variance between the standard (basic) amount and the comparable (actual) amount might be analyzed in stages, in that first the variance is analyzed (and attributed to variates) between the actual amount and a first intermediary standard amount, next the variance between the first intermediary standard amount and the second intermediary standard amount, and so on, until finally the variance is analyzed between the last intermediary standard amount and the (final, definitive) standard amount.

This analysis in stages may be of practical importance if we distinguish two stages, a short and a long term. Standard costs are established in the long term, based on production circumstances and price structures that are considered normal, and investment and other strategic decisions are based on them. Standard costs are the final standard of reference to which actual costs should be compared. However, in the short term, tactical considerations play a part and circumstances change. Short-term budgeted costs may differ from long-term standard costs, even if both are conceived as flexible budgeting curves rather than as fixed amounts. Thus we have two curves, the first of which is the long-term standard cost curve and the second the short-term budgeted cost curve differing from the first in any arbitrary way. Finally, the comparable amount is actual costs which must be conceived as an arbitrary point not necessarily on either curve.

Why should we analyze the difference between actual costs and standard costs in stages, first comparing actual costs to budgeted costs and next comparing budgeted costs to standard costs? Responsibility accounting provides the answer. Usually different persons in an organization are responsible for variables in the long term and the short term. For instance, market researchers and strategic planners may be responsible for long-term basic standards of output, whereas sales representatives and commercial managers may be responsible for achieving short-term budgeted targets; development engineers may be responsible for long-term standard factor usage per unit of output, whereas plant managers may be responsible for actually achieved, as compared to budgeted, factor efficiency. Hence, responsibility accounting requires a breakdown of total variance between actual and standard costs into a short-term partial variance between actual and budgeted costs, and a long-term partial variance between budgeted and standard costs. Then these partial variances may be further broken down and attributed to the variables involved.

A graphical illustration of the two-stage, two-dimensional variance analysis is given in figure 8.3. The point $A$ signifies actual costs, $B$ short-term budgeted costs, and $S$ long-term standard costs. The budgeted cost rate as a function of quantity produced is denoted by $R_B(Q)$, the standard cost rate by $R_S(Q)$. Figure 8.3 shows the case where all differences are positive, as in figures 8.1 and 8.2. The algebra of the breakdown, which is insensitive to the sign of the differences, is given in appendix 8.1.

The flexible-budgeting approach to variance analysis can also easily be extended to more than two dimensions. Since four and more dimensions are of little practical value in accounting variances, we restrict ourselves to the three-dimensional case. The algebra for the breakdown in the two-stage, three-dimensional case is given in appendix 8.2. We refrain from giv-

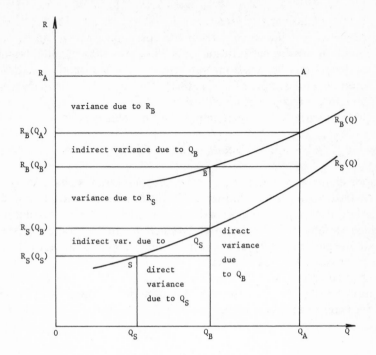

*Fig. 8.3.* Two-stage, two-dimensional variance analysis with flexible budgeting.

ing a three-dimensional graphical illustration; rather, we present a numerical example (in appendix 8.2).

Also in the three-dimensional case, the causal relationships are the basis used to attribute the partial variances to variables. Let the three-dimensional budgeted-cost model be denoted by

$$C_B = Q_B \times F_B \times P_B \tag{8.1}$$

where the subscript $B$ stands for budget, $C$ denotes costs, $Q$ quantity produced, $F$ factor usage per unit of output, and $P$ purchasing price per unit of the production factor concerned. It is essential that budgeted factor usage is considered a function of quantity produced:

$$F_B = F_B(Q_B) \tag{8.2}$$

and that budgeted purchasing price is considered a function of budgeted factor usage and quantity produced:

$$P_B = P_B(F_B(Q_B), Q_B) \tag{8.3}$$

Hence, $Q_B$ is cause and $F_B$ effect, and $F_B$ and $Q_B$ are cause and $P_B$ is effect, respectively. We thus have a recursive cost model which can be solved by simple successive substitution: substitute a numerical value for $Q_B$ in (8.2) and compute $F_B$; substitute numerical values for $F_B$ and $Q_B$ in (8.3) and compute $P_B$; and compute $C_B$ from (8.1). Thus there is a chain of variables beginning with $Q$ and ending with $P$.

The total variance between actual and budgeted cost is

$$C_A - C_B = Q_A \times F_A \times P_A - Q_B \times F_B \times P_B \tag{8.4}$$

Responsibility accounting requires that the total variance should be broken down into parts attributable to $Q$, $F$ and $P$. Flexible budgeting and the causal relationships in the recursive cost model conduce to attributing to a given variable the direct partial variance due to the difference between the actual and budgeted value of the variable as well as the indirect partial variances caused by the difference.

For a complete mathematical breakdown of total variance in the two-stage, three-dimensional case and for a numerical example of this case the reader is referred to appendix 8.2.

REFERENCES

[1]  G. Amerman, 'The mathematics of variance analysis', *Accounting Research* 4 (1953), 258–69 and 329–50, and 5 (1954), 56–79.

[2]  N. G. Chumachenko, 'Once again: the volume-mix-price/cost budget variance analysis', *Accounting Review* 43 (1968), 753–62.

[3]  N. Dopuch, J. G. Birnberg, and J. Demski, 'An extension of standard cost variance analysis', *Accounting Review* 42 (1967), 526–36.

[4]  C. R. Hasseldine, 'Mix and yield variances', *Accounting Review* 42 (1967), 497–515.

[5]  Ching-Wen Kwang and A. Slavin, 'The simple mathematics of variance analysis', *Accounting Review* 37 (1962), 415–32.

[6]  D. Lipsky, 'The dimensional principle in the analysis of variance', *NAA Bulletin* 42, nr. 1 (September, 1960), 5–18.

[7]  D. Solomons, 'Standard costing needs better variances', *NAA Bulletin* 43, nr. 4 (December, 1961), 29–39.

[8]  J. A. M. Theeuwes and C. B. Tilanus, 'De resultatenanalyse naar causale relatie', *Maandblad voor accountancy en bedrijfshuishoudkunde* 47 (1973), 14–26.

[9]  C. B. Tilanus and J. A. M. Theeuwes, *Variance analysis revisited.* Paper presented at the First European Congress on Operations Research, Brussels, 27–29 January 1975.

[10]  R. H. Watson, 'Two-variate analysis', *Accounting Review* 35 (1960), 96–99.

[11]  C. Weber, "The mathematics of variance analysis", *Accounting Review* 38 (1963), 534–39.

[12]  Z. S. Zannetos, 'On the mathematics of variance analysis', *Accounting Review* 38 (1963), 528–33.

# APPENDIX 8.1. Two-stage, two-dimensional variance analysis with flexible budgeting

Notation (see also figure 8.3 and ref. [9]):

$C$ a two-dimensional cost item
$Q$ quantity produced
$R$ rate of cost per unit of $Q$; arbitrary function of $Q$
$A$ subscript indicating actual
$B$ subscript indicating budgeted, short-term
$S$ subscript indicating standard, long-term

Breakdown of total variance:

$$
\begin{aligned}
C_A - C_S &= Q_A \times R_A - Q_S \times R_S(Q_S) \\
&= Q_A \times R_A - Q_B \times R_B(Q_B) \qquad \text{short-term part} \\
&\quad + Q_B \times R_B(Q_B) - Q_S \times R_S(Q_S) \qquad \text{long-term part}
\end{aligned}
$$

|  | partial variance attributable to: |
|---|---|

Breakdown of the short-term part:

$$
\begin{aligned}
Q_A &\times R_A - Q_B \times R_B(Q_B) \\
&= Q_A \times [R_A - R_B(Q_A)] \qquad\qquad R_B \\
&\quad + Q_A \times [R_B(Q_A) - R_B(Q_B)] \qquad Q_B \text{ (indirect)} \\
&\quad + [Q_A - Q_B] \times R_B(Q_B) \qquad\quad Q_B \text{ (direct)}
\end{aligned}
$$

Breakdown of the long-term part:

$$
\begin{aligned}
Q_B &\times R_B(Q_B) - Q_S \times R_S(Q_S) \\
&= Q_B \times [R_B(Q_B) - R_S(Q_B)] \qquad\qquad R_S \\
&\quad + Q_B \times [R_S(Q_B) - R_S(Q_S)] \qquad Q_S \text{ (indirect)} \\
&\quad + [Q_B - Q_S] \times R_S(Q_S) \qquad\quad Q_S \text{ (direct)}
\end{aligned}
$$

# APPENDIX 8.2. Algebra and numerical example of two-stage, three-dimensional variance analysis with flexible budgeting

Notation:

$C$ a three-dimensional cost item
$Q$ quantity produced
$F$ factor usage per unit of $Q$; arbitrary function of $Q$
$P$ purchasing price per unit of $F$; arbitrary function of $F$ and $Q$
$A$ subscript indicating actual
$B$ subscript indicating budgeted, short-term
$S$ subscript indicating standard, long-term

Breakdown of total variance:

$$C_A - C_S = Q_A \times F_A \times P_A - Q_S \times F_S(Q_S) \times P_S(F_S(Q_S),Q_S)$$

$$= Q_A \times F_A \times P_A - Q_B \times F_B(Q_B) \times$$
$$P_B(F_B(Q_B),Q_B) \qquad \text{short-term part}$$
$$+ Q_B \times F_B(Q_B) \times P_B(F_B(Q_B),Q_B) - Q_S \times F_S(Q_S) \times$$
$$P_S(F_S(Q_S),Q_S) \qquad \text{long-term part}$$

Breakdown of the short-term part:

partial variance attributable to:

$$Q_A \times F_A \times P_A - Q_B \times F_B(Q_B) \times P_B(F_B(Q_B),Q_B)$$

| | |
|---|---|
| $= Q_A \times F_A \times [P_A - P_B(F_A,Q_A)]$ | $P_B$ (direct) |
| $+ Q_A \times F_A \times [P_B(F_A,Q_A) - P_B(F_B(Q_A),Q_A]$ | $F_B$ (indirect) |
| $+ Q_A \times [F_A - F_B(Q_A)] \times P_B(F_B(Q_A),Q_A)$ | $F_B$ (direct) |
| $+ Q_A \times F_B(Q_A) \times [P_B(F_B(Q_A),Q_A) - P_B(F_B(Q_B),Q_B)]$ | $Q_B$ (2nd indirect) |
| $+ Q_A \times [F_B(Q_A) - F_B(Q_B)] \times P_B(F_B(Q_B),Q_B)$ | $Q_B$ (1st indirect) |
| $+ [Q_A - Q_B] \times F_B(Q_B) \times P_B(F_B(Q_B),Q_B)$ | $Q_B$ (direct) |

Breakdown of the long-term part:

partial variance attributable to:

$$Q_B \times F_B(Q_B) \times P_B(F_B(Q_B), Q_B) - Q_S \times$$
$$F_S(Q_S) \times P_S(F_S(Q_S), Q_S)$$
$$= Q_B \times F_B(Q_B) \times [P_B(F_B(Q_B), Q_B) -$$
$$P_S(F_B(Q_B), Q_B)] \qquad P_S \text{ (direct)}$$

$$+ \; Q_B \times F_B(Q_B) \times \left[P_S(F_B(Q_B),Q_B) - \right.$$
$$\left. P_S(F_S(Q_B), Q_B)\right] \qquad\qquad F_S \text{ (indirect)}$$
$$+ \; Q_B \times \left[F_B(Q_B) - F_S(Q_B)\right] \times$$
$$P_S(F_S(Q_B), Q_B) \qquad\qquad F_S \text{ (direct)}$$
$$+ \; Q_B \times F_S(Q_B) \times \left[P_S(F_S(Q_B), Q_B) - \right.$$
$$\left. P_S(F_S(Q_S),Q_S)\right] \qquad\qquad Q_S \text{ (2nd indirect)}$$
$$+ \; Q_B \times \left[F_S(Q_B) - F_S(Q_S)\right] \times$$
$$P_S(F_S(Q_S), Q_S) \qquad\qquad Q_S \text{ (1st indirect)}$$
$$+ \; \left[Q_B - Q_S\right] \times F_S(Q_S) \times$$
$$P_S(F_S(Q_S), Q_S) \qquad\qquad Q_S \text{ (direct)}$$

NUMERICAL EXAMPLE OF TWO-STAGE, THREE-DIMENSIONAL CASE

The ingredients are as follows (see also [8]):

$P_A$ = actual purchasing price per unit of
production factor    =    2.90
$F_A$ = actual factor usage per unit of output =    0.300
$Q_A$ = actual quantity produced    =    700
$Q_B$ = short-term budgeted quantity    =    800
$Q_S$ = long-term standard quantity    = 1000

The long-term and short-term functions for factor usage and purchasing price are given in tabular form in table 8.1. It is assumed that the product of $F$ and $Q$, total factor usage, forms the argument of $P$, hence

$$P(F(Q), Q) = P(F \times Q)$$

The total variance to be explained and to be attributed to short-term and long-term variables is (see also table 8.1):

$$700 \times 0.300 \times 2.90 - 1000 \times 0.200 \times 2.50$$
$$= 609.00 - 500.00 = 109.00$$

The short-term part is

$$609.00 - 800 \times 0.250 \times 2.80 = 609.00 - 560.00 = 49.00$$

The long-term part is

$$560.00 - 500.00 = 60.00$$

The further breakdown of total variance in partial variances attributable to individual short-term and long-term variables is given in table 8.2.

*Table 8.1.* Short-term and long-term tabulated functions for factor usage and purchasing price, numerical example.

| argument | | short-term functions | | | long-term functions | | |
|---|---|---|---|---|---|---|---|
| | $Q$ | $F_B$ | $F \times Q$ | $P_B$ | $F_S$ | $F \times Q$ | $P_S$ |
| | 1200 | .195 | 234 | 2.66 | .190 | 228 | 2.39 |
| | 1150 | .197 | 227 | 2.69 | .191 | 220 | 2.42 |
| | 1100 | .200 | 220 | 2.72 | .193 | 212 | 2.45 |
| | 1050 | .204 | 214 | 2.74 | .196 | 206 | 2.48 |
| $Q_S$: | 1000 | .210 | 210 | 2.76 | .200 | 200 | 2.50 |
| | 950 | .217 | 206 | 2.78 | .204 | 194 | 2.52 |
| | 900 | .226 | 203 | 2.79 | .210 | 189 | 2.54 |
| | 850 | .237 | 201 | 2.80 | .217 | 184 | 2.56 |
| $Q_B$: | 800 | .250 | 200 | 2.80 | .225 | 180 | 2.58 |
| | 750 | .264 | 198 | 2.81 | .235 | 176 | 2.60 |
| $Q_A$: | 700 | .280 | 196 | 2.82 | .250 | 175 | 2.60 |
| | 650 | .300 | 195 | 2.82 | .268 | 174 | 2.60 |
| | 600 | .325 | 195 | 2.82 | .290 | 174 | 2.60 |

*Table 8.2.* Two-stage, three-dimensional variance analysis with flexible budgeting, numerical example.

| partial variance attributable to: | factors based on the variable: | | | | result |
|---|---|---|---|---|---|
| | $Q$ | $F$ | $P$ | | |
| $P_B$ (direct) | $700$ | $\times 0.300$ | $\times 0.14$ | $= 29.40$ | |
| $F_B$ (indirect) | $700$ | $\times 0.300$ | $\times (-0.06)$ | $= -12.60$ | |
| $F_B$ (direct) | $700$ | $\times 0.020$ | $\times 2.82$ | $= 39.48$ | |
| $Q_B$ ($2^{nd}$ indirect) | $700$ | $\times 0.280$ | $\times 0.02$ | $= 3.92$ | |
| $Q_B$ ($1^{st}$ indirect) | $700$ | $\times 0.030$ | $\times 2.80$ | $= 58.80$ | |
| $Q_B$ (direct) | $(-100)$ | $\times 0.250$ | $\times 2.80$ | $= -70.00$ | |
| short-term part | | | | | 49.00 |
| $P_S$ (direct) | $800$ | $\times 0.250$ | $\times 0.30$ | $= 60.00$ | |
| $F_S$ (indirect) | $800$ | $\times 0.250$ | $\times (-0.08)$ | $= -16.00$ | |
| $F_S$ (direct) | $800$ | $\times 0.025$ | $\times 2.58$ | $= 51.60$ | |
| $Q_S$ ($2^{nd}$ indirect) | $800$ | $\times 0.225$ | $\times 0.08$ | $= 14.40$ | |
| $Q_S$ ($1^{st}$ indirect) | $800$ | $\times 0.025$ | $\times 2.50$ | $= 50.00$ | |
| $Q_S$ (direct) | $(-200)$ | $\times 0.200$ | $\times 2.50$ | $= -100.00$ | |
| long-term part | | | | | 60.00 |
| total variance | | | | | 109.00 |

# 9. Where short-term budget meets long-term plan

C. B. TILANUS

This article was inspired by difficulties arising in an industrial firm reconciling the budget with the long-term plan. It is said that 'the budget should be the first year of the long-term plan'. Yet conflicts between budget and plan are brought about by some obvious causes:

- Different people. Budgeting people usually have strong ties with the administration and day-to-day operation of the firm; long-term planners usually are way up close to top management.
- Different purposes. The budget is (still) mainly used for registration and control purposes; the long-term plan is used for major organizational and strategic decisions.
- Different procedures. The budget is typically made *bottom-up*. Information atoms on individual sales and cost items will be provided by commercial and production people on the spot. They will be more and more aggregated until finally the grand total is obtained. The long-term plan is typically made *top-down*. First, the strategic goals of the firm will be established, then the major qualitative and quantitative objectives will be determined, until finally a complete long-term plan emerges at a high degree of aggregation. In the time dimension long-term planning tends to work backwards: from the long-term goals to a medium-term plan and back to next year's budget. It is at this point that the difficulties arise.

The organization of this article is as follows. First we discuss the conflict between the budget and the first year of the long-term plan using a small numerical example. Then it is shown that the conflict can be solved using the latest available budget pattern and the aggregate figures from the first year of the long-term plan. The next section discusses the algorithm used for resolving the conflict (called the multiproportional RAS method). The final section points out that the algorithm is not as rigid as it seems, because all other specific prior information can be taken into account round about the RAS procedure.

## 9.1. NEXT YEAR'S BUDGET IN CONFLICT WITH FIRST YEAR OF LONG-TERM PLAN

Naturally, the budget for next year and that part of the long-term plan which refers to next year should tally. But if next year's budget is compiled bottom-up and the first year of the long-term plan is derived top-down, the odds are that they won't.

Yet both approaches have their merits. The bottom-up compilation of the budget ensures that full use is made of specific information of people on the spot concerning detailed items of the budget. This approach probably yields the pattern of individual budget items that is the most reliable. No warranty exists, however, against systematic errors made owing to general underestimation or, possibly, overestimation. The top-down long-term planning of aggregate totals focuses the attention to these totals and probably yields the most reliable forecasts of them. However, for a disaggregation of the first year's plan into a detailed budget additional information is needed[1]. It is suggested in this paper that this additional information be taken from the latest available budget.

Let us consider a small example. Table 9.1 gives the latest available sales budget for next year of a small firm. The budget distinguishes four products (A, B, C, D), three production locations (Rotterdam, Dusseldorf, Brussels), three markets (Benelux, Germany, World) and four quarters (I, II, III, IV). Thus it has four *dimensions*, viz., products, locations, markets, and time. Table 9.2 shows the budget's marginal totals for all four dimensions. The grand total sales figure is 90482. Table 9.3 gives the aggregates for next year directly estimated in the top-down long-term plan. According to this plan, the grand total sales figure is 108000, i.e. 19% more than the budget figure.

We assume that the budget *pattern* is reliable. However, there is a systematic tendency toward underestimation. We also assume that the long-term plan aggregate figures, being estimated directly, are the best available forecasts of marginal totals. How can we correct the budget to fit the long-term plan's marginal totals? Increasing all items of the budget by 19% will not help us because the marginal totals for the various dimensions all show up different ratios between the original budget and the long-term plan for next year. We want all marginal totals to tally.

## 9.2. USING BUDGET PATTERN FOR DISAGGREGATION OF LONG-TERM PLAN

In order to solve the conflict, the following assumption is made. Each item of the budget simultaneously changes proportionally to the corresponding

*Table 9.1.* Short-term bottom-up sales budget for next year.

| product | location | market | quarter I | II | III | IV |
|---|---|---|---|---|---|---|
| A | Rotterdam | Benelux | 1000 | 1200 | 1500 | 800 |
| | | Germany | 500 | 500 | 500 | 500 |
| | | World | 300 | 0 | 0 | 500 |
| | Dusseldorf | Benelux | 200 | 250 | 250 | 200 |
| | | Germany | 2000 | 2500 | 3000 | 2000 |
| | | World | 1000 | 500 | 0 | 1000 |
| | Brussels | Benelux | 600 | 800 | 700 | 500 |
| | | Germany | 200 | 200 | 200 | 200 |
| | | World | 2500 | 2000 | 2000 | 3000 |
| B | Rotterdam | Benelux | 100 | 200 | 300 | 400 |
| | | Germany | 200 | 200 | 200 | 200 |
| | | World | 2000 | 2500 | 3000 | 1500 |
| | Dusseldorf | Benelux | 100 | 100 | 100 | 100 |
| | | Germany | 400 | 600 | 800 | 1000 |
| | | World | 500 | 600 | 800 | 400 |
| | Brussels | Benelux | 600 | 800 | 1200 | 1500 |
| | | Germany | 200 | 300 | 400 | 500 |
| | | World | 5000 | 5500 | 6000 | 5000 |
| C | Rotterdam | Benelux | 1200 | 1000 | 1100 | 1200 |
| | | Germany | 300 | 100 | 150 | 200 |
| | | World | 150 | 150 | 150 | 150 |
| | Dusseldorf | Benelux | 600 | 500 | 400 | 200 |
| | | Germany | 1000 | 600 | 700 | 800 |
| | | World | 250 | 250 | 250 | 250 |
| | Brussels | Benelux | 300 | 300 | 200 | 200 |
| | | Germany | 100 | 50 | 0 | 50 |
| | | World | 150 | 75 | 75 | 50 |
| D | Rotterdam | Benelux | 25 | 35 | 45 | 20 |
| | | Germany | 10 | 12 | 12 | 8 |
| | | World | 25 | 30 | 15 | 20 |
| | Dusseldorf | Benelux | 8 | 8 | 8 | 8 |
| | | Germany | 65 | 75 | 100 | 50 |
| | | World | 20 | 20 | 25 | 25 |
| | Brussels | Benelux | 15 | 18 | 20 | 15 |
| | | Germany | 5 | 5 | 5 | 5 |
| | | World | 40 | 50 | 15 | 20 |

*Table 9.2.* Budget marginal totals for all four dimensions.

| product | | location | | market | | quarter | |
|---|---|---|---|---|---|---|---|
| A | 33100 | Rotterdam | 24207 | Benelux | 20925 | I | 21663 |
| B | 43300 | Dusseldorf | 24612 | Germany | 21702 | II | 22028 |
| C | 13200 | Brussels | 41663 | World | 47855 | III | 24220 |
| D | 882 | | | | | IV | 22571 |
| | 90482 | | 90482 | | 90482 | | 90482 |

*Table 9.3.* Long-term top-down sales plan for next year.

| product | | location | | market | | quarter | |
|---|---|---|---|---|---|---|---|
| A | 40000 | Rotterdam | 30000 | Benelux | 25000 | I | 24000 |
| B | 56000 | Dusseldorf | 18000 | Germany | 8000 | II | 24000 |
| C | 10000 | Brussels | 60000 | World | 75000 | III | 30000 |
| D | 2000 | | | | | IV | 30000 |
| | 108000 | | 108000 | | 108000 | | 108000 |

marginal totals. Thus each budget item in the example is subject to four 'multiproportional change factors', corresponding to the marginal totals for the product, the location, the market, and the quarter.

The multiproportional change factors are computed by an iterative procedure, called the multiproportional RAS method. It will be discussed in the next section. Results for our example were obtained after 5 CPU seconds on a Burroughs 6700 computer in 6 iterations. The speed of convergence may be indicated by the following series:

| percentage of initial sum of absolute marginal differences remaining after iteration: | | |
|---|---|---|
| number 0 | – | 100%   (= 117100) |
| number 1 | – | 24.85% |
| number 2 | – | 4.36% |
| number 3 | – | 1.08% |
| number 4 | – | 0.36% |
| number 5 | – | 0.12% |
| number 6 | – | 0.05% (= 56) |

The multiproportional change factors are given in table 9.4. To see how they are applied, let us consider the North-West element of table 9.1, sales of product A from location Rotterdam to market Benelux in quarter I, amounting to 1000. This figure should be multiplied by 1.427 (factor for product A) times 1.072 (factor for Rotterdam) times 0.959 (factor for Benelux) times 0.913 (factor for quarter I). The resulting figure is 1339, shown as the North-West element of table 9.5. Table 9.5 gives the complete budget after correction by the multiproportional change factors. Table 9.6

*Table 9.4.* Multiproportional change factors.

| product | | location | | market | | quarter | |
|---|---|---|---|---|---|---|---|
| A | 1.427 | Rotterdam | 1.072 | Benelux | 0.959 | I | 0.913 |
| B | 1.126 | Dusseldorf | 0.992 | Germany | 0.284 | II | 0.910 |
| C | 0.928 | Brussels | 1.032 | World | 1.254 | III | 1.063 |
| D | 2.835 | | | | | IV | 1.105 |

*Table 9.5.* Long-term top-down plan for next year disaggregated according to bottom-up budget pattern giving RAS-corrected budget.

| product | location | market | quarter I | II | III | IV |
|---------|----------|--------|-----|-----|-----|-----|
| A | Rotterdam | Benelux | 1339 | 1602 | 2338 | 1297 |
|   |           | Germany | 198 | 198 | 231 | 240 |
|   |           | World | 525 | 0 | 0 | 1060 |
|   | Dusseldorf | Benelux | 248 | 309 | 361 | 300 |
|   |           | Germany | 733 | 914 | 1280 | 888 |
|   |           | World | 1620 | 808 | 0 | 1961 |
|   | Brussels | Benelux | 773 | 1028 | 1050 | 780 |
|   |           | Germany | 76 | 76 | 89 | 92 |
|   |           | World | 4211 | 3359 | 3921 | 6118 |
| B | Rotterdam | Benelux | 106 | 211 | 369 | 512 |
|   |           | Germany | 63 | 62 | 73 | 76 |
|   |           | World | 2764 | 3445 | 4826 | 2510 |
|   | Dusseldorf | Benelux | 98 | 98 | 114 | 118 |
|   |           | Germany | 116 | 173 | 270 | 350 |
|   |           | World | 639 | 765 | 1191 | 619 |
|   | Brussels | Benelux | 610 | 811 | 1420 | 1847 |
|   |           | Germany | 60 | 90 | 140 | 182 |
|   |           | World | 6648 | 7292 | 9286 | 8049 |
| C | Rotterdam | Benelux | 1045 | 868 | 1115 | 1265 |
|   |           | Germany | 77 | 26 | 45 | 62 |
|   |           | World | 171 | 170 | 199 | 207 |
|   | Dusseldorf | Benelux | 483 | 402 | 375 | 195 |
|   |           | Germany | 238 | 143 | 194 | 231 |
|   |           | World | 263 | 263 | 307 | 319 |
|   | Brussels | Benelux | 251 | 251 | 195 | 203 |
|   |           | Germany | 25 | 12 | 0 | 15 |
|   |           | World | 164 | 82 | 96 | 66 |
| D | Rotterdam | Benelux | 67 | 93 | 139 | 64 |
|   |           | Germany | 8 | 9 | 11 | 8 |
|   |           | World | 87 | 104 | 61 | 84 |
|   | Dusseldorf | Benelux | 20 | 20 | 23 | 24 |
|   |           | Germany | 47 | 55 | 85 | 44 |
|   |           | World | 64 | 64 | 94 | 97 |
|   | Brussels | Benelux | 38 | 46 | 60 | 46 |
|   |           | Germany | 4 | 4 | 4 | 5 |
|   |           | World | 134 | 167 | 58 | 81 |

*Table 9.6.* RAS-corrected budget marginal totals.

| product | | location | | market | | quarter | |
|---------|--------|----------|--------|---------|--------|---------|--------|
| A | 40010 | Rotterdam | 30008 | Benelux | 25003 | I | 24000 |
| B | 55985 | Dusseldorf | 17998 | Germany | 8001 | II | 24000 |
| C | 10008 | Brussels | 59996 | World | 74998 | III | 30002 |
| D | 1999 | | | | | IV | 30000 |
|   | 108002 | | 108002 | | 108002 | | 108002 |

shows the marginal totals of the corrected budget. On comparing table 9.6 with table 9.3 it is seen that not only the grand total, but all budget marginal totals for the four dimensions tally sufficiently with the aggregate figures of the top-down plan.

### 9.3. THE MULTIPROPORTIONAL RAS ALGORITHM

In this section, the multiproportional RAS method is presented[2]. In order to keep the notation simple, the case of exactly four dimensions (as in the numerical example) will be dealt with. The general case of $k$ dimensions offers no new difficulties.

Let a four-dimensional array of budget items $\{a_{h,i,j,k}\}$ be given plus four vectors of marginal aggregates $\{mh_h\}$, $\{mi_i\}$, $\{mj_j\}$ and $\{mk_k\}$ of appropriate length. The problem is to find, using the multiproportional change assumption, four vectors of change factors $\{ch_h\}$, $\{ci_i\}$, $\{cj_j\}$ and $\{ck_k\}$ such that[3]

$$\sum_i \sum_j \sum_k a_{h,i,j,k} \cdot ch_h \cdot ci_i \cdot cj_j \cdot ck_k \approx mh_h \qquad \text{all } h$$

$$\sum_h \sum_j \sum_k a_{h,i,j,k} \cdot ch_h \cdot ci_i \cdot cj_j \cdot ck_k \approx mi_i \qquad \text{all } i$$

$$\sum_h \sum_i \sum_k a_{h,i,j,k} \cdot ch_h \cdot ci_i \cdot cj_j \cdot ck_k \approx mj_j \qquad \text{all } j$$

$$\sum_h \sum_i \sum_j a_{h,i,j,k} \cdot ch_h \cdot ci_i \cdot cj_j \cdot ck_k \approx mk_k \qquad \text{all } k$$

In the following algorithm, $\{b_{h,i,j,k}\}$ denotes an array which gradually converges to the required RAS-corrected budget array; $f$ denotes a working array of appropriate length; $=$ denotes the replacement operator where the direction is from right to left.

1. Check input data.
   There can be only one grand total; hence check whether

$$\sum_h mh_h = \sum_i mi_i = \sum_j mj_j = \sum_k mk_k$$

According to the multiproportional change assumption, zero elements in the original array are preserved in the corrected array. Thus the algorithm will fail if the original array has any zero marginal sum where the corresponding element of the marginal vector to which it should be adapted is positive. Check for this.

2. Initialization.

$$b_{h,i,j,k} = a_{h,i,j,k} \qquad \text{all } h, i, j, k$$
$$ch_h, ci_i, cj_j, ck_k = 1 \qquad \text{all } h, i, j, k$$

3a.
$$\left. \begin{aligned} &f_h = mh_h / \sum_i \sum_j \sum_k b_{h,i,j,k} \\ &b_{h,i,j,k} = b_{h,i,j,k} \cdot f_h \\ &ch_h = ch_h \cdot f_h \end{aligned} \right\} \qquad \text{all } h$$

3b.
$$\left. \begin{aligned} &f_i = mi_i / \sum_h \sum_j \sum_k b_{h,i,j,k} \\ &b_{h,i,j,k} = b_{h,i,j,k} \cdot f_i \\ &ci_i = ci_i \cdot f_i \end{aligned} \right\} \qquad \text{all } i$$

3c.
$$\left. \begin{aligned} &f_j = mj_j / \sum_h \sum_i \sum_k b_{h,i,j,k} \\ &b_{h,i,j,k} = b_{h,i,j,k} \cdot f_j \\ &cj_j = cj_j \cdot f_j \end{aligned} \right\} \qquad \text{all } j$$

3d.
$$\left. \begin{aligned} &f_k = mk_k / \sum_h \sum_i \sum_j b_{h,i,j,k} \\ &b_{h,i,j,k} = b_{h,i,j,k} \cdot f_k \\ &ck_k = ck_k \cdot f_k \end{aligned} \right\} \qquad \text{all } k$$

4. Check whether the process has converged sufficiently according to some criterion. For the computation of the example given in this paper the following criterion was used: the sum of all absolute differences between given aggregate figures and the corresponding marginal totals of the corrected array,

$$\sum_h \left| mh_h - \sum_i \sum_j \sum_k b_{h,i,j,k} \right| + \sum_i \left| mi_i - \sum_h \sum_j \sum_k b_{h,i,j,k} \right|$$
$$+ \sum_j \left| mj_j - \sum_h \sum_i \sum_k b_{h,i,j,k} \right| + \sum_k \left| mk_k - \sum_h \sum_i \sum_j b_{h,i,j,k} \right|$$

should be less than 0.1% of the same sum computed for the original array.

If the criterion is not yet satisfied, go to 3a.

5. Stop.

9.4. TAKING ACCOUNT OF PRIOR INFORMATION

It will not be proved here that the algorithm proposed converges. After all, the biproportional RAS method also was applied several years before it was proved that it worked[4].

In the problem discussed, it was assumed that the top-down long-term plan provided the best available forecasts of marginal totals aggregated over all dimensions but one. One can imagine that the long-term plan provides marginal totals aggregated to a lesser degree, viz., all but two or more dimensions. Here, we will not work out this case.

In this section, we will consider only one additional aspect, viz., the situation where one wants to take account of specific prior information with respect to individual budget items rather than apply to them the simple but mechanical RAS assumption of simultaneous proportional change. It is important to be able to make exceptions to the RAS rule, in order to increase the flexibility of the procedure. Fortunately, this feature can be easily dealt with. It is merely a matter of bookkeeping[5].

If one has superior *a priori* information about specific budget items or parts of specific budget items, all one has to do is:

– Wipe out these items or parts of items from the original budget array and subtract them from the corresponding marginal aggregates
– Apply the multiproportional RAS procedure to the remaining data
– Insert the specific items or partial items again into the corrected array to obtain final 'mixed' results.

It is hoped that the procedure presented here may help to bring the budgeting and long-term planning departments together without being afraid of the confrontation. It may certainly prevent a sub-optimal approach sometimes followed in practice, viz., compiling the long-term plan bottom-up for many years into the far future because no other possibility is seen to overcome disaggregation problems when the future comes nearer.

NOTES

1. This is also true in an information-technical sense. A more disaggregated breakdown contains more information than a less disaggregated one. For applications of measures borrowed from information theory in the social sciences see H. Theil, *Economics and Information Theory*, North-Holland, Amsterdam, 1967, and H. Theil, *Statistical Decomposition Analysis*, North-Holland, Amsterdam, 1972.
2. The original (biproportional) RAS method was proposed by R. Stone and J. A. C. Brown, in 'A long-term growth model for the British economy', a contribution to *Europe's Future in Figures*, editor R. C. Geary, North-Holland, Amsterdam, 1962. The name stems from the matrix product RAS, where A is a matrix to be corrected in accord-

ance with given marginal row and column totals, R is a diagonal matrix of row correction factors and S a diagonal matrix of column correction factors. Multiproportional RAS is a generalization of this method including the biproportional case.

3. Note that the number of degrees of freedom in determining the vectors of change factors is the number of dimensions less one. For if $\{a_{h,i,j,k} \cdot ch_h \cdot ci_i \cdot cj_j \cdot ck_k\}$ meets the constraints, then so does $\{a_{h,i,j,k} \cdot (ch_h \cdot \lambda_1) \cdot (ci_i \cdot \lambda_2) \cdot (cj_j \cdot \lambda_3) \cdot (ck_k/(\lambda_1 \cdot \lambda_2 \cdot \lambda_3))\}$ where the $\lambda$'s are scalars. The degrees of freedom may be used for some kind of normalization of the vectors, cf. M. Bacharach, *Biproportional Matrices and Input-Output Change*, Cambridge University Press, Cambridge, 1970.

4. See M. Bacharach, op. cit. See also C. B. Tilanus, *Input-Output Experiments*, Rotterdam University Press, Rotterdam, 1966.

5. The original biproportional RAS method was also extended in this way, cf. J. Paelinck and J. Waelbroeck, 'Etude empirique sur l'évolution de coefficients 'input-output'. Essai d'application de la procédure 'RAS' de Cambridge au tableau interindustriel belge', *Economie Appliquée* 16 (1962), 81–111.

# Index

Accounting
  cost - 109$n$
  financial - 109$n$
  responsibility - 147$n$
activity, dependent - 25$n$
AKZO 3
allocation
  cost - 96, 101
  overhead - 113
Amerman, G. 147, 154
analysis
  input-output - 134
  variance - 8, 147$n$
Anthony, R. N. 22
Argyris, C. 22
Arpan, J. S. 65
Ashby, R. W. 65
assortment, normal - 123$n$

Bacharach, M. 167
Backcharging 94$n$
Balas, E. 65
Baumol, W. J. 65
Benston, G. J. 134
Bertalanffy, L. von 65
Birnberg, J. G. 154
Bonini, C. P. 22
Bosman, A. 7, 134
Boulding, K. E. 65
Bouma, J. L. 7
Brooks, G. H. 134
Brown, J. A. C. 166
Bruns, W. J. 22
BS 44$n$
budget 1$n$, 10$n$, 82$n$, 109, 135$n$, 159$n$
budgeting 1
  - cycle time 2
  flexible - 2, 8, 147$n$
  interval - 135$n$
  quantitative - 85
  stochastic - 7, 135
Burroughs 162

Canning, R. G. 65
canonical experiment 146

Caplan, E. H. 15, 22
channel
  costing - 49$n$
  valuation - 50$n$
Ching-Wen Kwang 154
Chumachenko, N. G. 154
coefficient
  correlation - 20, 143
  technical - 98$n$, 110$n$
Conway, B. 65
co-production 24$n$
costs
  accumulated - 101$n$
  actual - 152$n$
  budgeted - 152$n$
  direct - 116$n$
  direct variable - 122$n$
  fixed - 147, 150$n$
  indirect - 116$n$
  opportunity - 112
  overhead - 113
  primary - 92$n$
  proportionally variable - 147, 150$n$
  semi-variable - 150$n$
  standard - 21, 113, 152$n$
  unit - 120$n$
  variable - 150$n$

Dearden, J. 22, 65
decomposition techniques 32$n$
De Coster, D.T. 22
De Finetti 146
degeneracy 32$n$, 48$n$
degrees of freedom 34, 47$n$, 141, 167
DeMasi, R. J. 65
Demski, J. 154
departments
  auxiliary - 85$n$
  production - 85$n$
dimension 71$n$, 151$n$, 160$n$
  measurable - 19$n$
distribution
  cumulative probability - 138
  - function 138$n$
  normal - 140

probability - 7, 137$n$
symmetrical - 137, 139
$t$ - 141
tabulated - 141
Dopuch, N. 154
DSM 3, 5, 7, 9, 92$n$
Du Pont 74, 91, 93
Dutch States Mines 5, 9, 92

Equation
balance - 27$n$, 122, 129
definition - 141
simultaneous - 7
Esso Nederland 3
ESTEL 3

Fabian, T. 65
factor
multiproportional change - 162$n$
production - 87$n$, 121
Fawthrop, R. A. 65
FORTRAN 75

GAMMA 4
Gauss curve 139
Gibbons, J. 65
Gordon, L.V. 13
Gozinto graph 133

Hass, J. E. 65
Hasseldine, C. R. 154
Hayes, R. H. 91
Hayhurst, G. 65
Hershey, R. L. 93, 108
Hofstede, G. H. 3, 4, 22
homogeneous, economically - 115$n$
Hopwood, A. G. 22
Horngren, C. T. 65
Human Relations 14, 21$n$

Ijiri, Y. 65
IMEDE 13
INTPRO 136, 140, 142

Johnston, J. 134

Klein Haneveld, A. 4, 65
Kloek, T. 7
Kreiken, J. 65
Krens, F. 65

Lach, E. L. 65
Lagrange multiplier 35
Lawrence, P. R. 22

Lipsky, D. 154
Lorsch, J. W. 22

Macko, D. 65
management by exception 16
matrix
band - 5, 9
costing - 55$n$
diagonal - 108, 111, 131, 167
end - 30$n$
identity - 118$n$
initial - 30$n$
Leontief - 6
non-singular - 124$n$
recompensing - 62$n$
rectangular - 7, 9
singular - 124
square - 9, 119
triangular - 6, 9, 98, 134
upper-triangular - 94
McDonald, D. L. 65
means of production 88$n$, 110$n$
durable - 112$n$
Mesarovic, M. D. 65
method
'American' 10
'European' - 10
interval budgeting - 135$n$
quantitative - 14$n$
Miles, R. E. 17, 22
Mize, J. H. 134
model
central - 40
corporate - 28, 78
input-output - 6$n$
management accounting - 15
mathematical - 17, 29, 74, 92
recursive - 6, 8, 154
Münstermann, H. 134

NB 43$n$
Netherlands 3, 7, 9
Netherlands Railways 8$n$, 135$n$
Nolan, R. L. 91

Objects
ancillary calculation - 26$n$, 50$n$
calculation - 24$n$
external ancillary - 51$n$
internal ancillary - 51$n$
linking - 26$n$
main calculation - 50$n$
optimization 12, 33, 74
Ostwald, P. F. 134

Paelinck, J.   167
period
  long -   126$n$
  medium -   126$n$
  short -   126$n$
Philips   3$n$, 9, 78
plan   109
  long-term -   8, 159$n$
  operational -   81
  period -   81
  project -   80
  short-term -   1
  strategic -   80
planning, strategic -   1, 126$n$
PPBS   1
principle, matching -   110
Pratt, J. W.   146
procedure, balancing -   40$n$
products
  end -   93$n$, 100$n$
  final -   114$n$
  intermediate -   93$n$, 98$n$, 114$n$
program, linear -   97
programming
  linear -   3, 7, 9, 26$n$, 74, 109$n$
  mathematical -   74

Raiffa, H.   146
RAS
  biproportional -   166$n$
  multiproportional -   9, 159$n$
ratio   5, 67$n$
  binary -   70
  - network   5, 9, 67$n$
reallocation   24$n$
recompensing   23$n$
relations
  algoristic -   41, 44$n$
  heuristic -   41, 44$n$
  normal -   41, 43$n$
Rhine-Schelde-Verolme   3
RHS   43$n$
Roberts, E. B.   22
roll-up   6, 9, 93$n$

Savage   146
Schlaifer, R.   146
Schroeff, H. J. v. d.   65
Schwartz, C. R.   93, 108
Shell, Royal Dutch/ -   3 , 4, 9, 23, 39
Shillinglaw, G.   65
simulation   7, 9, 74, 77, 140$n$
slack
  artificial -   29$n$
  individual -   30$n$

interrelation -   30$n$
  vacuous interrelation -   47$n$
Slavin, A.   154
Smits, H. A.   5
Solomons, D.   154
Stone, R.   166
suboptimization   12, 14
system
  budget control -   10$n$
  budgeting -   92$n$
  Mathematical Programming -   30, 44
  planning, programming
    and budgeting -   1
  socio-technical -   4, 11$n$
  total -   21, 28

Takahara, Y.   65
tariff   125
Theeuwes, J. A. M.   8, 154
Theil, H.   166
Thomas, A. L.   134
Thompson, G. C.   65
Tilanus, C. B.   8, 154, 167
transfer
  balanced - value   24$n$
  notional - price   32
  - price   23$n$
  - value   23$n$

Unilever   3, 7
Univac   93$n$, 96
Unterguggenberger, S.   65

Value, flow -   24$n$
Vancil, R. F.   22
Van der Donk, H. A.   7
Van der Enden, C.   4
variable
  endogenous -   68$n$, 109$n$
  exogenous -   68$n$, 110$n$
  flow -   70$n$
  mitigating -   40$n$
  pinning -   34$n$
  state -   70$n$
  stochastic -   142
  transfer -   40$n$
variance   10$n$, 84, 96, 147$n$
  accounting system -   12
  efficiency -   12
  expense -   12
  joint -   148
  quantity -   148
  rate -   148
  volume -   12
Vergin, R. C.   17, 22

Verheyen, P. A.   5
Verlage, H. C.   66
Vogel, F.   134

Waelbroeck, J.   167
Walker, W. E.   66
Watson, R. H.   154
Watts, D. E.   65

Weber, C.   154
White, C. R.   134
Wright, W. R.   66

Young, B. J.   66

Zannetos, Z. S.   154
Zionts, S.   58, 66